Thunderbolt Train Busters!

through to the front line. From the Germans' point of view, it was a case of keeping their front lines supplied with men and munitions.

The train busters' aim was to stop this, to save the lives of the Allies and of innocent people in occupied countries. This particular strategy hotted up towards the end of the war. Orders were made that all of the rail links in the German-occupied countries had to be cut.

The Americans with their P47d Thunderbolt planes set about this task efficiently. Armed with two 500lb. bombs and eight 0.5in. heavy machine-guns, they were deadly sky hunters.

The Thunderbolts would fly low until they caught a train on a bridge or causeway. Bombs in the back and bombs in the front knocked out the track. Then came more bombs or machine-gun bullets for the train.

At the height of the Italian campaign, groups of four planes would roam the country on these missions.

Probably the most bombed rail target in Italy during the war was the Arezzo Viaduct, an important link, on the inland route from Rome to Florence.

Many times was the line bombed — and rebuilt again.

But no sooner would it be repaired than a locomotive steaming along with troops or munitions would meet the fate you can see in our picture.

Sudden death at all times awaited the crews of these locomotives. When the Allied air forces gained the mastery of the air, their main job was to knock out all rail transport, to cripple the enemy.

They did so!

FOR VALOUR

The Victoria Cross

The guns had to be saved! It was bad enough for a British army to be beaten by the Boers, but to lose two entire field batteries of artillery was unthinkable. Now these guns lay out in the open South African countryside, only five hundred yards from the enemy's trenches. Around them the gun-crews and their teams of horses lay dead or wounded.

Suddenly a small band of officers and men galloped up from the British lines. A hail of bullets howled about them and shells tore the earth all around. Man after man fell as they struggled to limber up the stranded artillery until at last they managed to ride to safety with two guns. But the cost had been terrible and one of those who died was Lieutenant the Honourable Frederick Roberts. No less than seven Victoria Crosses were awarded that day, and one of them went posthumously to Lt. Roberts.

The Indian mutiny

This battle of Colenso, fought on December 15th 1899 during the Second Boer War, was a black day for Britain. It was also a sad day for Lord Roberts VC, who had now lost his son Freddie. Forty-two years earlier the old man had also won a Victoria Cross, during the Indian Mutiny, and although he must have been proud to hear that both he and Frederick had earned the highest of all their country's awards for bravery, nothing could repay him for the loss of his only son.

A memento

Wars had changed between these two events, however, and while Lord Roberts senior had fought his battle as a cavalryman, driving back mutinous sepoys with his sabre to save his squadron's flag, young Frederick Roberts had been forced to face modern rifles and rapid-firing artillery.

The gun that Lt. Frederick Roberts saved from the Boers at Colenso was later given to his father by the Government as a memento. Fourteen years later Field Marshal Lord Roberts, as he had now become, was still a soldier. Still serving his country he fell ill in France and died in November 1914. Yet that old gun still had its part to play, for it carried Lord Roberts' coffin during his funeral.

The Victoria Cross has always been one of the most difficult medals to win. As the years went by it seemed to get even more dangerous, which is why so many of those who earned the

VC did so posthumously. In fact, many people all over the world still regard the Victoria Cross as the greatest of all decorations for courage.

It was created by Queen Victoria in 1856, but was backdated to include the Crimean War. Until 1920 the Victoria Cross had two ribbons, dark red for the Army and blue for the Navy. Since then, however, the dark red ribbon has been used for all VCs. The bronze metal from which the crosses are made comes from a Russian cannon that was captured at Sevastopol in the Crimean War.

Only four civilians have won VCs. All others have been soldiers, sailors or airmen. Those lucky enough to survive, wear the medal in the position of honour before all other medals. In fact, only one medal can compete with the Victoria Cross and that is the George Cross. This was created in 1941 especially for civilians, since the VC has now been effectively reserved for servicemen.

It's impossible, it's incredible, but—

IT REALLY HAPPENED

1909—an early paysnatch ! Two ruthless crooks held up a motor car that was carrying wages to a nearby factory.

As the police rushed up, the bandits leapt aboard a tram and forced the driver to aid their getaway at gunpoint. The police commandeered a second tram and gave chase.

It was a long and exciting chase, but the police finally succeeded in capturing the two crooks.

Seaman Francis Schremp was securing cargo on the deck of a transatlantic ship during a storm when a gigantic wave swept him overboard.
For several agonising seconds he wallowed helplessly in the angry sea, sure that he was finished. Then another huge wave gathered strength and carried him to its crest. With all its fury, the wave hurled itself at the ship, and he found himself back aboard, safe once more!
Frenchman Charles Blondin, a famous 19th Century wire-walker, lived with danger. One of his most daring feats was to walk a wire suspended high above the Niagara Falls!
But a stunt like this was hungry work, so when he reached the middle, Blondin cooked himself an omelette over a small stove!

Karl Schaarschmidt, imprisoned for his many crimes, found himself locked in a small cell, with a thick wooden beam guarding the only way of escape.
But to Karl, anything was worth trying, and although he had no tools, he set about attacking the wooden bars of the window—with his teeth ! He worked for months, concealing his work with the dry bread fed to him by his captors.
It took him seven months to make the hole large enough to squeeze through, but his freedom was short-lived, for he was recaptured within a few weeks and returned to gaol.

CAPTAIN HURRICANE
IN 1941, THE GREEK AEGEAN ISLAND OF KARAVOS WAS OF MAJOR STRATEGIC IMPORTANCE TO THE ALLIES. INTELLIGENCE HAD LEARNED OF A PROPOSED GERMAN LANDING... AND CAPTAIN HURRICANE, WITH HIS PINT-SIZED BATMAN MAGGOT MALONE, HAD BEEN SENT THERE IN ADVAN VANCE, TO ORGANISE LOCAL DINGHY IN ADVANCE, TO ORGANISE LOCAL RESISTANCE...
BLISTERING BULWARKS! YOU'D THINK THEY'D HAVE SENT SOMEONE TO MEET US, TICH!
'ANG ON, SKIPPER— I CAN HEAR SOMETHING FROM THE VILLAGE! IT SOUNDS LIKE FIGHTING!
KLOBBA!
KLOBBA!
KLOD!
THAAAK!
YOU'RE FLIPPIN' WELL RIGHT, BY GLORY— ACTION! AND WE'RE MISSING IT! COME ON!
BUT AN AMAZING SIGHT MET THE MIGHTY MARINE'S EYES AS HE REACHED THE VILLAGE SQUARE!
THUNK!
KA-DUNGG!
KLODDA!
BONG!
SOAK ME IN SEAWEED! WHAT IN THUNDERIN' BLAZES IS THIS?
THEY— THEY'RE FLIPPIN' WELL DANCIN'!
AH! THE BRITISH SOLDIERS! JUST IN TIME TO WITNESS THE FAMOUS KARAVOS CLUB DANCE!
KLUNK!
WHICH ONE OF YOU HALF-WITS IS STAVROS?
THAT IS ME, MY CAPTAIN! I AM LEADER OF ZESE LION-HEARTED VILLAGERS!
WELL, YOU'RE WASTING YOUR FLAMIN' TIME DANCING WHEN YOU'RE ABOUT TO BE INVADED BY A LOAD O' KRAUTS! IT'S MY JOB TO GET YOU AND YOUR MEN TRAINED UP TO TACKLE 'EM!
TRAINING? WE NEED NONE! WIZ ZESE CLUBS, WE ARE DEADLY, MY FRIEND!
CLUBS? CLUBS? HOWLIN' HORNPIPES, IT'S GUNS AND GRENADES I'M TALKIN' ABOUT, PAL!

I AM SORRY, MY CAPTAIN! THERE ARE NO SUCH THINGS ON KARAVOS! BUT I ASSURE YOU, OUR CLUBS...!
ANGRILY, THE BIG MAN WENT BACK TO THE DINGHY TO USE THE RADIO...
THIS IS HURRICANE FROM KARAVOS! REQUEST AIRDROP OF RIFLES, AMMUNITION AND GRENADES, IMMEDIATELY! REPEAT... IMMEDIATELY!
THE MIGHTY MARINE HAD HARDLY FINISHED TRANSMITTING, WHEN...
AIEEE! ZE GERMANS HAF LANDED, BRITISH FRIEND! ON THE FAR SIDE OF ZE ISLAND! A WHOLE COMPANY, BY BOAT!
SUFFERING SARDINES, THAT'S ALL I NEED! BUT WEAPONS OR NO WEAPONS, WE'LL GIVE 'EM A BIT O' ONE-TWO!
LED BY A SCOUT, THEY SET OFF THROUGH THE MOUNTAINS...
'ERE, SKIPPER—I DON'T FANCY THIS! WE'VE ONLY GOT TWO BLOOMIN' GUNS BETWEEN US...!
DON'T WORRY, TICH! THE CHANCES ARE, WE'LL GET THE AIRDROP IN TIME!
BUT NEXT INSTANT...
FALL UPON THEM!
TEACH STAVROS AND HIS DOGS TO KEEP CLEAR OF OUR TERRITORY!
WHAT THE BARNACLE-BLISTERED BLAZES..?
WITH SECONDS, A BATTLE WAS RAGING!
IT IS COSTAS AND HIS MEN FROM A RIVAL VILLAGE IN THE HILLS, MY CAPTAIN! WE HAVE BEEN FEUDING FOR CENTURIES!
THUNK!
BASH!
KLOD!
THEN THIS IS WHERE THE FEUDING STOPS, YOU BUNCH OF HALF-BAKED GARLIC-GOBBLERS!
ORDER WAS SOON RESTORED—AND...
NOW LISTEN TO ME, YOU... SINK ME SIDEWAYS! WHAT IS IT, YOU MISERABLE WHELK?
ER-GERMANS, CAP'N! I THINK THE NOISE MUST'VE ATTRACTED THEM!
GAAH! I'M A PEACEABLE MAN, BUT THIS IS MORE THAN I CAN STAND! RUN, YOU MUNICH MUTTON-MUNCHERS, BEFORE I REALLY LOSE MY TEMPER!
RAT-TAT! TAT-TAT!
BACK! BACK FOR REINFORCEMENTS! THE GIANT IS NOT HUMAN!

AS THE ENEMY DISAPPEARED IN CONFUSION...
WELL DONE, MY CAPTAIN! COSTAS AND I WOULD LIKE TO CONGRATULATE YOU BEFORE WE RESUME OUR FEUD!
OO-ER! THE CAP'N AIN'T GONNA LIKE THAT!
THERE'S ONLY ONE THUMPIN' WAY TO GET SOME SENSE INTO YOU CLUB-CARRYIN' CLOWNS, AND THAT'S TO KNOCK IT IN!
BY THE STARS, HE IS RIGHT, COSTAS!
NOT EVEN THE ANCIENT CHAMPIONS OF OLYMPUS COULD EVER HAVE WITNESSED SUCH A FIGHT!
BIFF!
ZOK!
THA-DANGG!
SWOOOSH!
ZWISSHH!
AIEEEE! NEVER HAVE I SEEN ANYTHING LIKE IT!
AWWW, THIS 'APPENS ALL THE TIME, CHUM! YOU SHOULD SEE 'IM WHEN 'E REALLY GETS WORKED-UP!
URRGH! YOU ARE A MAN AMONG MEN, MY CAPTAIN!
NNNF! BY RIGHT OF COMBAT YOU ARE—OOOFF—LEADER OF US ALL!
GOOD! THEN LET'S GET CRACKIN' AND SORT OUT THOSE SAUSAGE-SWALLOWIN' SWABS BEFORE THEY JUMP US AGAIN!
WITH NO AIR-DROP YET IN SIGHT, THE BIG MAN RESORTED TO CUNNING...
RIGHT, TICH! WHEN THE SQUARE-HEADS SHOW UP, WE'LL DRAW 'EM DOWN TOWARDS US AGAIN THE GREEKS CAN COME DOWN FROM AMBUSH ON BOTH FLANKS!
AYE-AYE, SKIPPER! THOSE CLUBS'LL MAKE MINCEMEAT O' THE JERRIES!
CLUBS? DON'T MENTION THAT FLIPPIN' WORD, YOU DOZY LITTLE PRAWN! IF THERE WERE ANY OTHER WAY OF SCUPPERING THE BOOT-FACED BABOONS, I'D TAKE IT!
N-NOW K-KEEP YER 'AIR ON, SKIPPER!
THEY DIDN'T HAVE LONG TO WAIT. SUDDENLY, THERE WAS MOVEMENT AT THE FAR END OF THE VALLEY... AND THE ENTIRE GERMAN FORCE ATTACKED!
KEEP DOWN, TICH! THEY CAN'T SEE US! JUST DON'T FIRE UNTIL THEY'RE WELL IN...!
RAT-TAT! TATTA-TAT!

AT THAT MOMENT...
STRIKE ME PINK, CAP'N! IT'S OUR AIR-DROP!
STAVROS SAW IT TOO... AND WAS UNABLE TO RESTRAIN HIMSELF!
YA-HEEEE! TAKE THEM, MY BROTHERS!
STOW MY FLAMIN' HAMMOCK!
THE CLUB STRUCK THE ASTONISHED GERMAN'S GUN EVEN AS HE UNLEASHED A WILD BURST...
RAT-TAT! TAT-TAT!
KLUNK!
YAAAGGH!
AND THE BULLETS FOUND THE CRATE OF PARACHUTED ARMS!
BAROOMPA!
FOR A MOMENT, THERE WERE ONLY THE ECHOES OF THE EXPLOSION... BUT THEN THE VALLEY SHOOK AS THE MIGHTY MARINE ERUPTED INTO A SPECTACULAR "RAGIN' FURY"!
WHIRLING WINDJAMMERS! I'M SOCKED AROUND WITH STICKS, PLAGUED BY A PAIR O' PUNCH-HAPPY PARTISANS, SHOT AT BY SWAGGERIN' SQUAREHEADS... AND NOW ALL ME AMMO GOES UP IN A PUFF O' PERISHIN' SMOKE! WELL, IT'S TIME I LOST ME FLAMIN' TEMPER!
AAAAGH! THE ENGLANDER HAS GONE BERSERK!
EEEE!
KAMERAD!
SURRENDER!
I'LL BOUNCE THE WHOLE BUNCH BACK TO BERLIN, SO HELP ME!
THE ISLANDERS WERE QUICK, AND EAGER TO USE THEIR CLUBS... BUT THEY WEREN'T QUICK ENOUGH!
BY THE STARS, IT IS NOT FAIR! NOT ONE LITTLE TINY HEAD LEFT TO HIT!
HIMMEL!
KLUNG!
YEEARGH!
THAT'S THE SKIPPER ALL OVER, MATE! ANYONE WHO WANTS TO JOIN HIS KIND OF CLUB 'AS TO ENLIST IN THE ROYAL MARINES! HA! HA!

FOR VALOUR The Medal

Israel's little Piper Cubs didn't look very military, but these "Primus Stoves", as they were called, were for a while the most powerful aircraft in the Israeli Air Force. During the civil war between Arabs and Jews in Palestine the Arab villagers had nothing with which to resist these Pipers, with their racks of 20 kilogram bombs. By June 1948, however, the situation had changed. The British had given up trying to control Palestine and had left. The Zionists had declared their independence as the state of Israel and the neighbouring Arab states had marched in to help the beleaguered Palestinian Arabs.

More warlike planes were rapidly pouring into Israel, but the new Israeli Air Force still had to use its old Piper Cubs. In June 1948 Zvi Ziebel flew one such aircraft with a cargo of weapons to the Israeli settlement of Ben Shemen. Now, on June 25th, he was trapped. His little aircraft lay in the middle of a field, under fire from a neighbouring Arab village.

"Tank"

Suddenly the young pilot had a brainwave. A few minutes later Zvi Ziebel emerged from the farm buildings driving a tractor piled high with sand-bags. As enemy rifle-fire buzzed around him, the Israeli pilot parked this improvised "tank" between the Arabs and his Piper Cub.

Unfortunately, there was still another problem. A large rock lay some way in front of his plane, but this time Zvi Ziebel could not hide behind his tractor. Instead the pilot ran out into the open, shifted the obstacle and raced back to the sand-bags. Still the enemy's fire crisscrossed the field, but now he had to take off. With the throttle wide open, the Piper Cub leapt from behind the sheltering tractor, hurtled across the field and clawed its way into the air.

Never claimed

Almost exactly six months later Ziebel's luck finally ran out. The savage war between Arabs and Israelis had changed, but although the Israeli Air Force now flew Spitfires, Mustangs and Messerschmitts, some men still had to fly the old Piper Cubs. One of these was Zvi Ziebel, and on December 27th he and another Israeli light aircraft were caught over Beersheba by a flight of Egyptian fighters. Most of the Egyptian pilots in Sinai still had to use outdated Mark 9 Spitfires. A few, however, flew new Fiat G 55s. Either type of fighter was enough to shoot Zvi Ziebel's little Piper Cub from the sky, but for some reason the destruction of Ziebel's aircraft was never claimed by an Egyptian pilot. Perhaps the victor was Pilot Officer Said. On that same day he was himself shot down not far

for Valour

away by a Canadian fighter-ace who was flying as a mercenary for the Israelis.

Recognised

More than twenty years passed before Zvi Ziebel's bravery was recognised. He was then posthumously awarded one of Israel's new Medals of Valour. These were instituted in 1970 for acts of supreme heroism, and could only be awarded by the Minister of Defence on the personal recommendation of the Chief of Staff. Twelve Israelis earned Medals of Valour in the Palestine War of 1948. Zvi Ziebel was the only pilot among them, and as such he was one of the first men to win one of the world's newest awards for courage.

As enemy rifle-fire buzzed, the Israeli pilot parked his "tank" between the Arabs and his Piper Cub.

The Policeman Who Caught Himself!

Chief Inspector Robert Ledru of the Sûreté was puzzled when he put his socks on one summer morning and found that they were damp. The previous evening he had arrived at the Normandy port of Le Havre to work on a new case and had gone to sleep early, with his revolver beneath his pillow.

He had no time to puzzle out what had happened to his footwear — his shoes also appeared to have been out in the wet — and he hurried off to introduce himself to the local police.

Murder

Ledru had been sent to Le Havre to solve the mysterious disappearance of some seamen in the area. But on reaching the police station he was told that his case was now of secondary importance. There had been a brutal murder during the night and it was hoped that he, Ledru, would help to try and solve it.

Proprietor

The victim was a middle-aged man named André Monet, the proprietor of a Paris dress-shop, who had recently come to the coast for the good of his health. His body had been found on the beach that dawn. He had been killed by a bullet which had passed right through his body.

Intrigued by the killing — for which there appeared to be no reason, motive, or suspect — Ledru went to investigate the scene of the crime. Eyes on the alert, he walked along the sandy beach to the spot where the corpse had been discovered.

The detective noticed a set of footprints leading up to and away from the dead man and stopped to examine them. When Ledru arose his face was troubled and he ordered that plaster casts be made of the marks.

"They look familiar to me," he said. "I seem to have seen them somewhere before."

Ledru spent the rest of the morning gazing at the plaster casts — which he took to a remote part of the beach and studied as if they were about to reveal something vital to him.

Solved

Finally, as the waters of the English Channel began to lap around his feet, Ledru stood up and strode over to the mystified gendarmes. "There is no need to stay here any longer," he declared. "The case is solved. I know the identity of the killer!"

Without another word, he hurried back to his hotel, where he remained locked in his room. He did not emerge until the following morning, when he went to see the chief of the Le Havre police. The chief informed the detective that the fatal bullet had been picked up on the beach. "Good," said Ledru. "That is the final piece of evidence I need. May I see it?"

The bullet was handed to him and he took out his revolver. He noted that a round had been fired, and compared the recovered bullet with the one in an unfired cartridge.

"Just as I thought," he said dramatically. "You need look no further for your killer. He is right here. *I* am the man who shot Monsieur Monet!"

At the age of 35, Ledru was famed as the man who caught murderers and who opposed all violent law-breakers. He had made his name in Paris, where he had broken up black magic cults and had arrested scores of anarchists. Three years earlier, in 1884, he had enjoyed one of his greatest triumphs, when he had tracked down and seen imprisoned a group of political rebels who planned to overthrow the government.

Dedication

It was this unswerving dedication to stamping out crime, that prompted Ledru to name himself as an apparently cold-blooded and ruthless killer. With the plaster casts and death bullet in his possession, he took the next train to Paris, where he reported to his superior at the Sûreté. He poured out the story of the body on the beach and related that the victim had been shot by a German pistol.

"My own gun is of German make," he admitted. "And, indeed, is the murder weapon itself."

Reconstruction

Ledru reconstructed the murder stage by stage. The killer, he said, had woken up in the middle of the night and put on his socks, shoes and clothes. He had then left his first-floor bedroom by the window and had made his way to the beach, with its long stretches of sand and rock-pools. There he had come across Monsieur Monet taking a midnight stroll and had, it seems, got into conversation with him.

"I'm not sure what was said," went on Ledru. "Perhaps the killer asked too many questions and the men quarrelled. Perhaps Monet unintentionally annoyed or upset him. Who knows? All I do know is what happened next. And it was this . . ."

The moment he spotted a set of footprints leading to the murder victim, Inspector Ledru was struck with the strange feeling that he knew to whom they had to belong.

Ledru then described how the killer drew his gun, shot the Parisian through the chest, and left the victim to die. The murderer hurried back to his home, hotel or lodging-house, climbed in through the window, returned the gun to its hiding place, and went to bed.

"I don't think the murderer knew what he was doing," said Ledru in conclusion. "I believe that he was walking in his sleep and committed the murder while in a trance. The man is sick, very sick, and could easily kill that way again. Which is why I insist that I be arrested and put somewhere where I can do no more harm."

Fantastic

At first, the heads of the Sûreté found it difficult to believe Ledru's fantastic story. But gradually, as the evidence was once again examined and pieced together, they came to believe that he had indeed killed in his sleep.

He was said to be suffering from too much work and too many mental problems, and was imprisoned for his own good. While in jail he was given a pistol loaded with blanks and a close watch was kept on him day and night.

Then, one midnight, Ledru rose while still asleep, took the gun from under his pillow, and fired at point-blank range at one of his guards. This convinced the authorities that he had been telling the truth, however unbelievable it sounded.

From then until his death in 1937, Ledru lived in seclusion on a farm outside Paris. He was watched over by doctors and armed personnel, to whom he sometimes told the weird, true-life story of the detective who caught himself.

Galloping Dick

It was a bitterly cold night and Dr. William Roots had not relished the journey from Putney to the Bald Faced Stag, a lonely inn on the Portsmouth Road. But he was comforted by the fact that his visit had been providential. The young stranger — he could not yet be 20 years old — was certainly very sick, and the doctor had bled him according to the medical practice of that time, the 1790s.

The patient was most grateful for all the doctor's efforts and, when the medical man was about to leave, earnestly entreated him to be on the watch for highwaymen.

"You had better, sir, have someone to go back with you, as it is a dark and lonesome journey," he said.

Doctor Roots declined his patient's thoughtful suggestion with a snort, asserting, "I have not the least fear, even should I meet with Abershaw himself."

Dr. Roots was at a loss to understand why the young man found this remark so hilarious. One wonders whether the good doctor would have seen the joke had he known that this young man he had been treating was none other that the most feared and celebrated highwayman of his day, Jerry Abershaw.

Louis Jeremiah Abershaw was born in 1773 at Kingston, Surrey. He took to the road early and, at 17 years of age, became captain of a band of highwaymen who infested what are now the southern suburbs of London.

During one of his stays in London, Abershaw and one of his companions were out on the Great North Road when they encountered a chaise. Donning their masks, the highwaymen rode up to the postilion and commanded him to stop. There was a strong wind blowing and a sudden gust blew off Abershaw's crepe mask. The postilion and the highwayman stared at each other and Abershaw saw the look of recognition in the other's face. Before either could speak there were sounds of horses approaching and the two highwaymen galloped off.

Worried about the postilion having recognised him, Abershaw decided to wait at an inn where the chaise was expected to stop and attempt to buy the man's silence. The postilion accepted the bribe and further agreed to meet the highwayman later for supper. Over good food and drink, the postilion, whose name was Ferguson, agreed to become Abershaw's confederate.

This new alliance was at once a great success, and any number of unsuspecting travellers, driven by the innocent-looking young postilion, found themselves being held up by a pair of masked riders.

After some time, Ferguson himself took to the road though his skill in the saddle saved him from capture many times.

Jerry Abershaw was becoming a thorn in the side of the Bow Street Runners, who felt that not being able to catch him was ruining their good name. But early in 1795, the runners received a tip-off that Abershaw was in the habit of frequenting an inn called the Three Brewers in Southwark. A round-the-clock surveillance was then placed on the hostelry.

After several days their vigil was rewarded and Abershaw was seen entering the Three Brewers. Throwing open the door, two runners burst in to arrest the highwayman. But Abershaw was, as ever, on the alert and he leapt from his chair, a pistol in each hand. Disregarding the highwayman's threat to shoot if they came any nearer, the runners advanced. Abershaw fired both pistols simultaneously.

One shot hit and mortally wounded one of the officers, David Price, while the other ball went wide and struck the landlord, Bernard Turner. With both his pistols discharged, Abershaw was soon overpowered.

On 30th July, 1795, Jerry Abershaw was tried at Croydon Assizes for the murder of David Price, the Bow Street Runner. Although a legal technicality invalidated this charge, he was eventually found guilty of felonious shooting and sentenced to death. So contemptuous was Abershaw of the court's proceedings that, when the judge assumed the black cap to pronounce sentence of death, the highwayman donned his own hat.

Several gaolers had to struggle with him while he hurled abuse at judge and jury. Finally, his hands had to be manacled and bound before he could be carried from the dock.

On 3rd August, 1795, Abershaw was taken in a cart to be hanged on Kennington Common. Like most of the highwaymen he showed no fear. A flower in his mouth and his shirt open at the neck, the young highwayman (he was only 22) laughed and nodded to the vast crowd.

Arriving at the gallows Abershaw kicked off his boots. This, he shouted to his audience, was to disprove his mother's prophecy that he would die with his boots on. This implied that he would come to a villain's end by execution and not die of old age or illness in bed.

After he had been hanged, his body was gibbetted on Putney Common, scene of his chief exploits. Thousands of Londoners went to see the dangling corpse of the last truly notorious "gentleman of the road."

The Fisherman who caught an Island

According to Maori legends, New Zealand was created thousands of years ago by a young Maori fisherman called Maui. The original inhabitants of New Zealand, the Maoris, have a legend about how their country was created.

The legend says that a god named Maui was fishing with his brothers far to the south of their homeland. Suddenly he hooked something. A titanic struggle ensued, but Maui triumphed. From the depths he brought up the North Island of the country we call New Zealand. The Maoris called it Te Ika a Maui, "The Fish of Maui."

Folk-lore

The story of the Maoris before the coming of the white man is steeped in myth and folk-lore. We know only fragments of their past, stories handed down by the mouths of trained tribal historians — for the Maoris had no written language. When the great seaman and explorer Captain Cook got to know them, he called them "a brave warlike people with sentiments devoid of treachery". The British soldiers who fought against them regarded them more highly than any other native opponent they ever encountered. How could you fail to admire men who sometimes sent you food so that the battle could continue, or who asked for extra ammunition so that the fight could go on longer?

"Moahunters"

The Maoris who still live mainly on North Island, were not the first people to inhabit New Zealand, however. Archaeologists call the earlier people "the moahunters", since they were a race who hunted the moa — a huge, now extinct bird as big as a man — sometimes bigger. But the birds and the people who hunted them had vanished long before the Maoris arrived some time in the 14th century. Some scholars believe that they came from the islands of Tahiti and its neighbours. While traditional Maori sources have the first settlers arriving around AD 825, today's Maoris believe that they are descended from colonists who arrived in the 14th century.

The land they found was not as easy to live off as their homeland, but they planted sweet potatoes and yams and cleared some of the forests. Although they do not seem to have had iron or metal, they were gifted workers in wood, as their weapons, ornaments, houses and canoes show.

Fortress

In all, there were probably a quarter of a million of them, divided into tribes that lived in villages consisting of long, ornately-constructed houses. Near most villages was a fortress called a pa. Usually situated on a hilltop, they were surrounded by ditches and had tree trunks forming an impenetrable palisade.

The Maoris formed close-knit communities. Each tribe was led by a chief, while at the bottom of the social ladder were the slaves, most of whom were taken as prisoners in bitter tribal wars. They believed in several gods, the most powerful of whom was the supreme deity Io.

One of their best-known superstitions was the idea of tapu, the word which became "taboo" in England and came to mean "unspeakable" or "prohibited". Tapu was a spell which could be cast to protect a tribal chief, or private property, such as the burial grounds of the dead. To break the spell by touching or trespassing on the things protected by tapu would result in sickness, and even death, brought on by the actions of the gods.

The Maoris loved public debates, but undoubtedly their favourite activity was fighting. They fought fierce hand-to-hand combats with spears, clubs and throwing sticks.

Warlike

It looked as if nothing would disturb their way of life. Though warlike, they were an artistic and civilised race. Suddenly, however, they were faced with something more potentially destructive than any of their gods — the white man. These two races were one day able to come together to form one of the world's most stable and admirable nations.

He Hated Hold-Ups

James Maclaine's hands shook every time he robbed a coach. The moon was shining brightly one November night in 1749 when a carriage carrying Horace Walpole, Earl of Orford, the famed writer, was crossing London's Hyde Park.

Suddenly a horseman cut across the coach's path and compelled the startled driver to stop. At the same time, another horseman rode up alongside the carriage and thrust his pistol through the window. The earl found himself staring into the masked face of a highwayman.

The masked robber seemed to be suffering from an acute case of nerves — indeed Walpole noticed to his alarm that the pistol in the highwayman's hand was shaking. The next instant the pistol flashed with a loud report and a ball grazed the skin beneath Walpole's eye, blackening his face with powder and leaving him stunned. The nervous highwayman and his companion then proceeded to relieve the unfortunate traveller of his belongings.

The name of the highwayman who had fired the pistol was James Maclaine, while his partner was a man called Plunkett. It seems that Maclaine was most upset by the incident, for he wrote two letters of apology to Horace Walpole.

In his letters, he said that if he had killed Walpole he would have taken his own life. To prove his remorse the highwayman offered to meet Walpole one night at Tyburn and give him back some of the stolen property. Although Walpole was most impressed by Maclaine's civility, he did not take up his offer.

James Maclaine had been born in Ireland in 1724, the son of a Presbyterian minister who was descended from a noble Scots family. By the time he was 18, both his parents had died and young James was left a legacy of nearly £1,000 — which he immediately squandered on riotous living in Dublin.

Fortunately for the young man, he was introduced to a wealthy landowner who needed a butler. James's gentlemanly appearance and charming manner got him the job and he travelled to London with his master. He was soon dismissed, but he once again fell on his feet by marrying the daughter of a rich horse-dealer and publican.

With his wife's generous dowry James opened a grocer's and chandler's shop. Three years later, however, his wife fell ill and died, and Maclaine sold the business.

It was then that he decided upon a course which was to lead him to the gallows. He determined to invest all his money in a short period of fashionable living with the objective of finding and marrying a wealthy woman. He took rooms in St. James's Street at tremendous expense and was seen at all the most fashionable places wearing splendid clothes. His capital soon dwindled, however.

He therefore went to an apothecary friend named Plunkett for help. Plunkett decided to invest some of his capital in Maclaine's fortune-hunting and also to act as his servant. The two men agreed that when a successful marriage had been obtained Plunkett would be given a well-paid position in Maclaine's household.

It was not long, however, before Plunkett's capital was eaten up as well. So, in order to finance their scheme, the apothecary suggested a desperate course of action: they would take to the road.

One evening shortly afterwards, Maclaine found himself much against his will, masked and mounted with a pistol in each hand, concealed with Plunkett in the shadows beside the road running through Hyde Park.

Soon a lone horseman appeared, and Maclaine and Plunkett rode out to accost him. Plunkett levelled his pistol and ordered the traveller to "stand and deliver!" Suddenly Plunkett realised he would have to conduct this robbery alone — for Maclaine had retreated a few paces and sat too terrified to move!

However, this first attempt at highway robbery was financially successful and it became the first of many. They decided to attack the St. Albans coach, Maclaine riding out to force the driver to rein in the horses while Plunkett rode up to the coach and robbed the passengers.

At least, that was the plan.

When the moment came to attack, Maclaine became so frightened that he dug his spurs into his horse and galloped wildly off across the fields, leaving Plunkett to handle the robbery himself.

Despite Maclaine's nervousness, the pair became very successful highwaymen. Their career, however, was not to last long.

In the summer of 1750, while badly in need of money, Maclaine decided to sell some of his large wardrobe. Unfortunately, one of the items he sold was a coat and waistcoat that had been widely advertised as stolen. The clothing was quickly recognised and Maclaine was arrested.

The highwayman immediately confessed everything, at the same time attempting to put all the blame on his partner, Plunkett. That canny gentleman, however, was never seen or heard of again.

At the Old Bailey, Maclaine cut a dashing figure. He was attired in the height of fashion, concealing his manacles as best he could with large lace cuffs. He called numerous witnesses to his good character, but he was found guilty and sentenced to death.

Horace Walpole had never lost his interest in the highwayman who had nearly taken his life. He wrote that on the first Sunday after Maclaine's conviction, more than 3,000 people visited his cell at Newgate. The enormous crowd were moved to tears to see the handsome "Gentleman Highwayman" awaiting his end in the condemned cell.

An appointment with the General

The Mexican and the American needed each other, for a fortune in gold was their common aim. But could they trust each other?

"D'you want the job or not? It's dangerous, but the pay makes the risks worth while." The man who spoke was burly, but anyone who thought the loose-fitting jacket covered fat would be making a mistake. The jacket was drawn back to reveal the butt of a revolver slung low on its holster. There were no notches in the butt. He was not the sort of man who bothered to remind himself of the number of men who had faced him.

The tall handsome Mexican seated across the bar room spoke in a low voice.

"Let me get this straight, gringo. You say that Generale Pascale will be transporting a fortune in gold bullion from Los Ventros to his headquarters. You know the route he will take and the date. You want me to help you get that bullion and you will pay me 10,000 dollars. Right?"

The burly man let his eyes drift slowly round the cantina. Americans, although not unusual in this part of Mexico, were not popular. It was no accident that the seat he had chosen had its back to the wall.

"Right."

"But why me? I don't know you. I've never clapped eyes on you in my life."

"Mebbe. But I've seen you, Ramon Guarez — in Portros."

The Mexican's eyes suddenly narrowed. Slowly, almost imperceptibly, his hand slid towards the knife in his belt.

"Yeah, I've seen you," continued the American lazily. "I was in Portros the day you escaped from the military fort — the day before you were due to face the firing squad!"

The Mexican's hand closed on the handle of the knife.

"I wouldn't use that if I was you," drawled the American. "You're probably very quick — but not so quick that you can beat a bullet from the Derringer in my pocket pointing straight at your belly.

"Stop and think. Didn't you ever wonder how the guard *happened* to turn his back so conveniently and gave you the chance to grab him through the bars of the cell? Was it just coincidence that he happened to have the keys in his belt instead of on the wall where they were usually kept? And do you reckon it was just chance that there was a saddled horse waiting outside the rear gate of the fort?"

A puzzled frown creased the Mexican's forehead.

"You mean *you* . . .?"

"Sure. I figured it was worth a few hundred dollars in bribes to get you out of that fort. I reck'oned a man who was going to be shot on the orders of your dear dictator General Pascale might not have too much love for him. And I needed someone who could get the men necessary to handle this job."

A heavy silence fell between them. A thousand questions raced across the Mexican's face. His eyes never left those of the American.

"I do not trust a gringo."

"And I don't trust a Mex."

For another thirty seconds the two men stared at each other. Then abruptly, the Mexican's shoulders relaxed. His white teeth gleamed in a smile. He held out his hand.

"All right, gringo. We have a deal."

The American took the proffered hand. His other hand stayed in his pocket

"We shall need twenty men. You pick them and offer them a thousand dollars each — paid when we complete the job. We meet in the canyon south of the town at dawn on Wednesday. Be ready for a three-day ride. Adios, amigo!"

The Mexican accepted his dismissal. The grin remained on his face as he rose to his feet.

"Adios, amigo!"

He sauntered slowly through the cantina and passed through the swing-doors. For five minutes the American stayed in his chair with his back to the wall. Then he too crossed the floor and slid into the night.

The sun was nosing over the mountains as the American rode slowly towards the band of Mexicans gathered in the canyon. They watched him with wary eyes. In the early years of the 20th century Americanos who crossed the Rio Grande, the river that formed the border between Texas and Mexico, were usually men on the run from the United States' authorities. Usually they brought trouble. But for a thousand dollars . . .

If the American was aware of the hostility he gave no sign of it. Silently he scanned the group, taking in their weapons, their horses. Then he nodded to Guarez.

"Let's go."

It was dusk before the group halted outside the little village of Quantro. All day they had ridden south through the foothills, avoiding roads and used trails.

"We'll stop here for the night," said the American to Guarez. The going gets tough from now on."

"Does that mean we are heading into the mountains?" asked Guarez.

"Mebbe. Just grab your sleep while you can. I'll be in the hotel. We leave at dawn."

The American prodded his horse and without a backward glance headed towards the lights of the village.

There were three men in the little cantina. They were playing cards with a greasy deck. The American gave them a brief glance before he took a chair with his back to the wall and ordered food.

He was drinking his third cup of coffee when the door burst open and six of the Mexicans from the group rushed in, their rifles aimed straight at him. The card players blinked nervously, then rose from their table and shuffled to the side of the room.

"Don't make one move, gringos," hissed the leader of the group. "Six rifles cannot miss at this range."

The American slowly drained his cup.

"I wouldn't dream of moving. In any case, it's your move. You hold the rifles."

The leader of the group advanced cautiously, and a rifle butt thudded against the American's head.

"Si, gringo, and we will use them if we have to."

He grabbed the American's hair and pulled him upright. The rifle pressed against his temple.

"Now you talk, gringo. You tell us where the bullion is coming and when. We do not share any fortune with filthy Americanos."

The American sneered contemptuously.

"Vamoose, Mex. No one gets any details from me until I'm ready to give 'em."

The Mexican's eyes glinted angrily. His finger tightened on the trigger. *"Drop that rifle!* And the rest of you, too!"

All heads swivelled. At the top of the stairs Guarez crouched behind a machine gun which poked through the bannisters and pointed into the middle of the group.

For what seemed an eternity no one moved. Then the nose of the machine gun tilted slightly upward and a spray of bullets thudded into the far walls of the cantina. Sullenly, the Mexicans dropped their rifles and gazed with hate-filled eyes as Guarez slowly descended the stairs, the heavy machine gun rock-steady in his arms. He reached the bottom and gestured towards the door.

"Outside!" he ordered.

The six Mexicans glanced apprehensively at each other, then slowly, reluctantly, they began edging towards the door. Guarez followed them.

A silence descended on the cantina. The card players cautiously returned to their table with sidelong looks at the American. He sipped at his tequila. Suddenly the rattle of a machine gun filled the air. Then silence again!

Footsteps echoed on the wooden sidewalk outside, and Guarez walked in. He no longer had the machine gun. He grinned at the American, noting the hand hovering over the holstered gun.

"I am sorry about that, amigo. One cannot trust anybody these days. But do not worry. They will give you no more trouble. They will not give *anyone* any more trouble. Buenos noches. Sleep well!"

There were only 14 in the group that awaited the American next morning. Guarez greeted him cheerfully.

"Buenos dias, amigo. We head for the mountains, si?"

The American did not answer. Instead he pulled on his horse's head and pointed him eastwards, away from the mountains. Guarez shrugged his shoulders, then jerked his head for the rest of the band to follow.

They were prepared for another hard, day-long ride and they could not conceal their surprise when after an hour the American dismounted.

They were in a small valley nestling between gently-sloping hills, with boulders scattered here and there. A dried-up stream meandered through the centre of the valley, leaving a narrow path on either side.

"This is where the bullion will come."

Guarez looked around him incredulously. The American had gone mad. True, the boulders would give his men protection but it would take the army accompanying the bullion a matter of minutes to deal with fourteen. The same thought occurred to the rest of the Mexicans. They began muttering among themselves.

The American ignored them. From his saddle-bags he produced a number of sticks of dynamite, which he proceeded to place in a shallow hole scraped in the ground and cover with a thin layer of sand. Then he unwound a thin length of wire, unreeling it slowly as he backed towards one of the boulders. He connected the end of the wire to a detonator. Only then did he face the men.

"Take up your positions behind the boulders," he barked. A rare smile crossed his face. "And don't worry.

I know what I am doing."

For several moments the men hesitated. Their eyes turned to Guarez. And only when he nodded did they move towards the sheltering rocks.

An hour passed. Then a rumbling could be heard in the distance. The Mexicans glanced uneasily at each other. The American indicated to them to get down.

The noise grew louder. And then, travelling slowly over the uneven ground, a single lorry appeared at the end of the valley. Crouched behind a boulder, the American waited, his hands on the plunger of the detonator. As the front wheels of the lorry passed over the shallow hole in the ground, he pressed the plunger home.

The lorry reared into the air as the dynamite exploded, then crashed back to earth again. Flames began to engulf it, and six soldiers hurled themselves out into the sand. From the boulders a hail of bullets whined through the air and two of the soldiers fell. The remainder dropped their rifles and held their arms in the air, alarm and disbelief battling each other on their faces.

"Hold your fire!" roared the American.

Then another figure emerged from the cabin of the lorry, his hands high above his head. A fat man with heavy jowls, he wore a bright green uniform adorned with gold epaulettes and braid. A red sash crossed one shoulder. A gold-encrusted cap sat on his greasy black hair. Normally his eyes were cold and cruel. Now they were wide with fear.

"General Pascale!" hissed Guarez. He lifted his rifle.

"Drop it!" snarled the American, his Colt pointing unwaveringly at the Mexican's head. Only a few yards separated them, the rifle and the revolver now pointing directly at each other. Death was poised in those few yards as the two fingers crooked round the triggers.

It was Guarez who lowered his rifle. He opened his mouth to speak, then suddenly turned on his heel and joined his men, now frantically heaving the heavy, bullion-filled boxes from the blazing lorry. The whiteness on the American's knuckles disappeared as he relaxed, but he did not return his gun to its holster as he moved towards the sweating, peacock-clad figure staggering away from the lorry.

Within an hour the gold had been transferred to the saddle-bags. The Mexicans could scarcely believe their luck. Never had they seen so much wealth, never had they acquired money so easily. They grinned happily as they lifted the heavy boxes. Only Guarez wore a frown.

"Tell me, amigo," he said to the American resting his back against a boulder, "why was the Generale travelling without a full military escort? Normally he does not move anywhere unless he has a hundred men with him. And how is it that an Americano on the run comes to know of such things?"

The American glanced at the quivering dictator seated with his hands tied behind his back a few yards away.

"The Generale may be a coward, but he's no fool. He knew it was only a matter of time before someone would oust him — and he wasn't waiting. That gold was going to his own private hideaway. And you don't take an army escort with you when you aim to flee the country.

"Pascale ruled by fear. But you can only keep people oppressed for so long — until a natural leader comes on to the scene, a leader who can unite the people to overthrow that oppressor. I hear such a man has come along. As to how I know about such things, well, that will just have to remain my little secret."

It was the longest speech Guarez had heard the American make. He rose to his feet and sauntered towards his horse tethered behind the boulder. The American took a pouch of tobacco and paper from his pocket and began to roll a cigarette. A hammer clicked behind him and he felt the barrel of a revolver pressed against the back of his neck.

"I am sorry about this, amigo," said Guarez softly. "But I am afraid you are not going to have that gold. I have other plans for it. That money was stolen from the people. It is going back to the people."

The American slid his cigarette along his tongue.

"I know."

The pressure of the gun lifted fractionally. Then Guarez eased round the boulder until he faced the American. The gun remained steady, a few inches from the burly man's forehead.

"Why don't you put that gun down?" drawled the American. "You know you're not going to use it. And while you're at it why don't you call the six men hiding at the end of the valley? The six men you supposedly killed with the machine gun!"

Guarez was obviously startled.

"How did you know that I didn't shoot them?" he asked.

"When a man is going to shoot you with a rifle," said the American, "he doesn't put the safety catch on!" He smiled at the Mexican's discomfiture. "But why was all that charade necessary?"

Guarez stepped back a pace, the revolver lowering uncertainly.

"I did not trust you — and I knew you did not trust me. I also knew that you were not the sort of man who would talk under the threat of death. But by pretending to rescue you I figured you would think I was only interested in getting my 10,000 dollars and therefore would be on your side." He shrugged his shoulders. "And should anything go wrong, should you double-cross us, well, at least there would be six men left to deal with you and see that the gold would get to its rightful owners — my people."

Neither man spoke for a few minutes. Then the American broke the silence.

"The gold is yours, Guarez. It was always intended for you. I said that a people would remain oppressed until a man came along to lead them in their fight. It was no accident that I picked *you* to come on this raid. I know you will rule this country well and wisely."

The American produced a small leather wallet.

"You see, I never wanted the gold. But I did want Pascale. And I wanted him back in America. A year ago Pascale crossed the border to organise some gun-smuggling. While he was there he shot a man in the back and killed him. That man's name was Allan Grant. I swore to take his killer back to face justice."

The American held out the wallet for Guarez to take. The Mexican flipped it open. "John Grant," he read, "U.S. Government Agent."

Guarez raised his eyebrows in an unspoken question.

"Allan Grant was my brother," the burly man said.

A while later the men were mounted in two groups. The main group moved away slowly, the gold weighing heavily in their saddle-bags. Four Mexicans were in the other group with the American and General Pascale.

"They will see that you reach the border safely," said Guarez. He held out his hand and grinned.

"Never trust a Mex?"

"Never trust a gringo?"

The two men gripped each other's hand firmly. Then Grant pulled on his horse's head and turned northwards, ex-General Pascale bouncing behind him.

CAPTAIN HURRICANE
IN JULY 1943, THE ALLIES INVADED SICILY, AND SOON AFTER THE LANDINGS, CAPTAIN HERCULES HURRICANE'S UNIT OF ROYAL MARINE COMMANDOS WAS ORDERED TO ATTACK AND CAPTURE A HILL-TOP CASTLE WHICH WAS BEING STRONGLY DEFENDED BY ITS GERMAN GARRISON...
COO, THE WHOLE PLACE LOOKS PEACEFUL ENOUGH FOR A PICNIC, CAP'N! MAYBE THE SAUSAGE-NOSHERS ARE ASLEEP!
THEN LET'S WAKE 'EM UP! WE'LL TRY A FRONTAL ATTACK UP THE PATH TO THE MAIN GATES!
CHAAARGE! STAND BY TO BE DOUBLE-CLOBBERED, YOU DOZY, DACE-FACED DEUTSCHERS! THE ROYALS ARE HERE IN FORCE!
HAH! NOT A SINGLE SHOT SO FAR, SKIPPER! MEBBE THE PRUSSIAN PERISHERS 'AVE PULLED OUT COMPLETELY!
BUT HURRICANE'S PINT-SIZED BATMAN, MAGGOT MALONE, WAS WRONG! FOR SECONDS LATER...
F-TOOM!
KER-RUMP!
NAAARGH!
BLISTER MY BILGES, THERE'S A MORTAR TEAM DUG IN ON OUR RIGHT FLANK! TAKE COVER!
TICH, CLIMB TO THE TOP OF THOSE THUMPIN' ROCKS! USE THE BREN TO SPRAY THE KRAUTS WHILE WE ADVANCE UP THE PATH OUT OF RANGE OF THAT FLAMIN' MORTAR!
WHUMPF!
AYE, AYE, CAP'N! I'LL KEEP THEIR BLOOMIN' 'EADS DAHN!
MOMENTS LATER, THE LITTLE BATMAN WAS IN POSITION. AND...
IT'S WORKING, BY THUNDER! WEIGH ANCHOR, ME HEARTIES... ADVANCE!
RAT-TAT! TATTATT!
SPIANG!
HIMMEL!
FOR TEN MINUTES, MAGGOT STUCK GRIMLY TO HIS TASK... BUT THEN HIS ATTENTION BEGAN TO WANDER!
'ELLO, THERE'S A TINY LITTLE FLOWER GROWIN' IN THAT CRACK! NOW I WONDER WOT MIRACLE O' MOTHER NATURE MANAGED TER GET A SEEDLIN' RIGHT UP 'ERE AN' TAKE ROOT—?

WAAAW! SWIPE ME SIDEWAYS THROUGH SMITHFIELD MARKET! I'VE GORN AN' DROPPED THE BLINKIN' BREN!
KER-R-ANG!
PRAANG!
FREED FROM MAGGOT'S WITHERING FIRE, THE GERMAN MORTAR TEAM LEAPT INTO ACTION ONCE AGAIN, AND...
GNAAGH! WE'RE PINNED DOWN LIKE DUCKS IN AN ICED-UP POND, CAP'N! MAGGOT MUST 'AVE COPPED IT!
THE DOZY SPRAT IS MORE LIKELY TO BE HAVIN' A CRAFTY RIP! PULL BACK, SHIPMATES! RETREAT!
BLAAM!
KER-WUMP!
BLACK-FACED WITH RAGE, THE MIGHTY MARINE LED HIS MEN BACK OUT OF RANGE. THEN...
ANOTHER FLAMIN' MESS-UP! WHAT HAPPENED THIS TIME, YOU GORMLESS, GUPPY-FACED EXCUSE FOR A FIGHTING MARINE?
I-ER- SORT OF LOST ME GRIP ON THE BREN, CAP'N... AN' BENT IT A BIT!
GRRR-RRR! YOU'RE AS USELESS AS A HADDOCK IN A HAYLOFT, YOU HALF-WITTED LITTLE HA'PORTH! WHEN I GIVE AN ORDER, I EXPECT IT TO BE CARRIED OUT! D'YOU UNDERSTAND?
Y-Y-YES, S-S-SKIPPER!
FROM NOW ON, YOU'LL OBEY MY EVERY COMMAND TO THE LETTER... OR, SO HELP ME, I'LL BOOT YOU ALL THE BLISTERING WAY FROM HERE TO BRINDISI!
BOOT!
RIGHT, YOU 'OLLERIN' GREAT 'ULK, I'LL DO JEST THAT! I'LL SHOW YER WHETHER I CAN TAKE BLINKIN' ORDERS OR NOT!
DARKNESS FELL... AND CAPTAIN HURRICANE DECIDED ON A NEW PLAN OF ATTACK...
WE'RE GOING TO TRY AND SCALE THIS FLAMIN' CLIFF AT THE REAR OF THE CASTLE, SHIPMATES! THE BLACK-BREECHED BUCKET-HEADS WILL NEVER EXPECT AN ASSAULT FROM THIS DIRECTION!
A TOUCH OF THE MOUNTAIN GOATS, EH, CAP'N? GOOD IDEA..!
BUT I SUGGEST YOU POST A COUPLE OF SENTRIES UPSTREAM A BIT—JUST IN CASE THE KRAUTS PATROL THIS PATH FROM TIME TO TIME!
JUMP TO IT, MALONE! PICK THREE MEN AND GET UP THERE! AND I WANT BAGS OF HUSH TOO, UNDERSTAND?
YES, SAH!
RUST MY RUDDER, THE SAP-BRAINED SCALLOP IS ACTING LIKE A REAL MARINE FOR ONCE! MAYBE THAT LECTURE I GAVE HIM HAD SOME THUMPIN' EFFECT!
BUT MOMENTS LATER, MAGGOT RETURNED, CRASHED TO ATTENTION ONCE AGAIN, AND...
MARINE MALONE REPORTING BACK, SAH! ONE REQUEST CARRIED OUT AS ORDERED, SAH!
HUU-UUH? WHAT THE BLAZES ARE THOSE SUPPOSED TO BE, YOU BLENNY BRAINED BARNACLE?

BAGS OF 'USH, SAH! THREE OF 'EM TER BE EXACT! FILLED TER THE BRIM WIV STILL NIGHT AIR! THE QUIETEST KIND Y'CAN GET... SAH!
WHY, YOU MUTINOUS, MEALY-MOUTHED, MICKEY-TAKING SON OF A MINCE-FACED MEAT-GRINDER, I'LL...!
BANG!
POP!
STONE ME, YOU'VE BURST THE BAGS, CAP'N! THEY SOUNDED LIKE RIFLE SHOTS—THE KRAUTS WILL HAVE HEARD THOSE BANGS FOR SURE!
FAR ABOVE, THERE WAS THE CLANG OF AN ALARM BELL. THEN...
FSSSHT!
FZZT!
FLARE!
FLARE!
FLARES! THAT'S DONE IT NOW!
WELL, BEAT ME ON THE BONCE WITH A BLISTERING BLANCO BRUSH!
ZUNK!
BLANCO BRUSH? CERTAINLY, CAP'N!
GNN—AAOW!
SINK... SINK ME S-SIDE-WAYS!
YES, SAH! SIDEWAYS IT IS!
SPLAASH!
GLOOOO-GAAARG!
EYES GLAZED, CAPTAIN HURRICANE ROSE FROM THE WATER LIKE AN ENRAGED HIPPOPOTAMUS...
GRR-RRR! Y-YOU'VE DONE IT, THIS TIME, MALONE! I'LL KEEL-HAUL YOU FOR MUTINY! MAKE YOU WALK THE FLIPPIN' PLANK THEN TIE YOU BY THE TOES TO THE HIGHEST THUNDERIN' YARDARM I CAN FIND!
BEGGIN' YER PARDON, CAP'N, BUT YOU BLOOMIN' WELL WON'T! YOU TOLD ME—IN FRONT O' WITNESSES—THAT I 'AD TO OBEY YER COMMANDS TO THE LETTER! AN' THAT'S JUST WOT I'VE BEEN DOIN', SO THERE!
AS THE TERRIBLE TRUTH SUNK IN, THE BIG MAN EXPLODED INTO ONE OF THE MOST AWESOME, VOLCANIC "RAGIN' FURIES" OF ALL TIME!
GREAT SUFFERIN' SEA-SLUGS! I'M A SERVING OFFICER IN THE ROYAL MARINES, AND WHAT FLAMIN' WELL HAPPENS? A SAWN-OFF SWAB OF A BATMAN HANDS ME PAPER BAGS FULL OF BLISTERING AIR, BASHES ME WITH A BLANCO BRUSH, THEN SINKS ME SIDEWAYS IN A MOUNTAIN STREAM... AND THERE'S NOT ONE THUNDERIN' THING I CAN DO ABOUT IT!

WELL, SO HELP ME, IF I CAN'T COURT-MARTIAL THAT CRAFTY, COD-FACED LITTLE CLOWN, I'LL CLIMB UP AND CLOBBER SOME CABBAGE-CRUNCHERS, INSTEAD! GRRR!
KRAK! KRAK!
RAT-TAT-TAT TATTAT!
PEEOING!
ACHTUNG! ACHTUNG! A MAD ENGLANDER ATTEMPTS TO SCALE DER CLIFF! CUT HIM DOWN!
KRAAK!
SPAANG!
GAH, HE MUST HAF DER NINE LIVES, LIKE A CAT! THE DOLT STILL KOMMS UPWARDS!
THAT'S RIGHT, FRITZY! UPWARDS!
ZINNGG!
THUKKA! THUKKA!
CHUNK!
KRAK!
... AND INWARDS!
GDNNNG!
KRR-UMP!
GAAOWWFF!
BIFF!
HIMMEL!
ZONK!
YEOWW!
WHAM!
GAAARGH!
ZAMM!
STRIKE ME PINK, THE SKIPPER'S PUNCHED A GREAT BIG 'OLE IN THE CASTLE WALL! LET'S GET UP THERE AN' GIVE 'IM A HAND, SHIPMATES!
I DOUBT IF 'E BLOOMIN' WELL NEEDS ONE! HE'S TAKIN' ON THE WHOLE GARRISON SINGLE-HANDED!
AND SURE ENOUGH, WHEN THE MARINES REACHED THE TOP OF THE CLIFF...
NEEARGH!
SWIPE ME, HE'S WRAPPIN' UP THE LAST FOUR SAUSAGE-NOSHERS IN THEIR OWN FLAMIN' FLAG! THE BATTLE'S OVER! THE CASTLE'S OURS!
GROOAGH!
TOO FLIPPIN' TRUE, ME HEARTIES! WHICH IS A PITY, 'COS I WAS JUST BEGINNING TO ENJOY MY THUMPIN' SELF!
GRINNING CHEEKILY, MAGGOT STEPPED FORWARD...
MARINE MALONE REPORTING AGAIN, SAH! ARE THERE ANY OTHER ORDERS YOU'D LIKE ME TO CARRY OUT TONIGHT, CAP'N?
YES, JUST ONE, YOU MICKEY-TAKING LITTLE MICROBE...!
GET LOST!
YAAAOW!
BWUMP!
HA, HA! SERVES YOU RIGHT, MAGGOT! THE BOOT'S ON THE OTHER FOOT NOW, AS Y'MIGHT SAY!

FOR VALOUR

The Order of

Captain Izzat was determined that his mission should succeed. But it meant endangering his life longer than instructed. Was it worth it?

Bale Out — these were the standing orders in such a situation. Pilots were far more valuable than planes to the Egyptian Air Force in September 1968 and although aircraft could be replaced, highly trained men could not. Egypt possessed far fewer aircrew than did the Israeli Air Force and even if they were captured they would, eventually, be returned to their units.

Captain Hussein Izzat knew his orders. He also knew that he was alone over Sinai, except for the four Israeli Mirage fighters that had jumped him east of the Mitla Pass. His chances of survival should have been nil, but Izzat was not a man to give up so easily. He had taken his lumbering Su-7 deep into enemy-held territory on a photographic reconnaissance mission. Maybe this hadn't been a suicide sortie, but it had been dangerous enough. In that summer of 1968 the Israeli Air Force ruled the skies over the Egyptian province of Sinai. The entire area had been occupied in the Arab-Israeli June War of the previous year — a war in which the Egyptian Air Force had been totally crushed. Nevertheless, Capt. Izzat had reached his target, which lay almost at the limits of his Sukhoi's range. He had taken his vital photographs and now he intended to get them home.

When the four Israeli Mirages pounced, Izzat threw his aircraft down almost to ground level. By hugging the desert he confused the enemies' heat-seeking missiles, for the sands of Sinai were almost as hot as the Sukhoi's exhaust. Now mountains reared before him, but Hussein Izzat still kept as low as possible and flew through a bleak and rocky pass. The Mirages followed and tried to hit the Egyptian plane with cannon-fire, but as all five aircraft twisted and turned between the jagged rocks, the Israelis could not keep the Sukhoi in their sights.

Safe

Suddenly the thin blue line of the Suez Canal flashed beneath Capt. Izzat's wings and a barrage of anti-aircraft fire erupted between him and his pursuers. The Su-7 and its precious photographs were safe.

Not surprisingly Captain Hussein Izzat earned the Order of the Military Star for his daring flight. He was the first Egyptian pilot to win this medal since Egypt's humiliating defeat in June 1967. The Air Force was, in fact, the last of the country's three armed services to regain its self-respect. The Army had done so in "Operation Rescue" which saved Egypt's last toe-hold in Sinai, Port Fuad, from enemy occupation, while the Navy did so by sinking Israel's flag-ship "Eilat" in October

the Military Star

1967.

The Order of the Military Star, which was won by Capt. Izzat, is one of the oldest decorations in the Middle East. Although there are other medals that can be given to all the ranks, this Star is reserved for officers and for "distinguished deeds of sacrifice in the field of battle". It was first instituted as the Military Star of King Fuad I in 1919, but after the Egyptian Revolution of 1952, the medal's name was changed to the Order of the Military Star. The basic design remained the same, however, except that its original crown and crossed swords were replaced by republican emblems. An Ancient Egyptian hawk was also added to the clasp, but the bright yellow and blue ribbon of the Military Star is unchanged.

CAPTAIN HURRICANE AND STEEL COMMANDO
IN 1944, BRITAIN'S MOST INCREDIBLE SECRET WEAPON—THE STEEL COMMANDO—WAS SENT WITH THE MAN WHO COULD CONTROL IT, LANCE-CORPORAL ERNIE "EXCUSED BOOTS" BATES, TO JOIN CAPTAIN HERCULES HURRICANE'S UNIT OF ROYAL MARINE COMMANDOS. NOW IN BELGIUM, AND POISED FOR A FINAL THRUST AGAINST THE GERMAN DEFENCES, HURRICANE WENT LOOKING URGENTLY ONE DAY FOR HIS PINT-SIZED BATMAN . . . MAGGOT MALONE . . .
AVAST THERE, MALONE, YOU WALL-EYED SON OF A BOW ROAD BELL-RINGER! WHERE THE BLUE BLISTERING BLAZES ARE YOU?
PELIKAAN STRAAT
IN 'ERE CLEANIN' YER KIT, CAP'N! AN' I'M UP TO ME BLOOMIN' NECK IN BLANCO AN' BOOT POLISH!
THEN DROP EVERYTHING AND COME WITH ME! THAT BAG O' WIND BATES HAS BEEN ORDERED INTO THUNDERIN' SICK BAY FOR A WEEK!
GAH! TRUST THAT SKIVIN' PERISHER TER WANGLE 'IS TICKET! WOT'S 'E GOT THIS TIME . . . COLD FEET?
NO! A DOSE O' THUMPIN' FLU! THE ROACH-FACED RUNT IS SHIVERIN' AND SHAKIN' LIKE A BUTTERFLY IN A BLIZZARD!
R·A·P
OOO-ER! SO 'E IS! SERVES 'IM RIGHT FOR WALKIN' ABOUT BELGIUM WIVOUT BOOTS!
AYE, SO WITH BATES OFF SICK, YOU'LL HAVE TO BE IN CHARGE OF THE STEEL COMMANDO FOR THE NEXT SEVEN DAYS, TICH!
I-I'VE JEST FINISHED ALTERING THE VOICE-TAPES . . . SNUFFLE . . . MAGGOT! UNTIL I'M BETTER, IRONSIDES WILL OBEY ONLY YOU! SAY . . . SNURFFLE . . . SOMETHIN' AN' SEE WOT 'APPENS!
ER . . . UM . . . HAND ME THAT THERE BLOOMIN' RIFLE, IRONSIDES! SHARPISH-LIKE!
YES . . . MAGG-OT!
EYES FLASHING, THE STEEL COMMANDO TURNED, AND . . .
WELL, BASH ME BOGGLE-EYED WIV A BLOATER . . . IT BLINKIN' WELL WORKED!
OF COURSE IT FLAMIN' WELL WORKED, YOU GORMLESS GUPPY! NOW YOU HAVE TWENTY FOUR HOURS TO GET REALLY FAMILIAR WITH OPERATING THE STEEL COMMANDO . . . !
. . . BECAUSE AT 1700 HOURS TOMORROW, WE MOVE AGAINST A KRAUT OIL REFINERY NEAR THE BORDER! OUR ORDERS ARE TO BLOW THE PLACE TO BITS — AND I WANT YOU AND THAT THUMPIN' TIN-MAN IN CLOSE SUPPORT!
YES, SAH! YOU CAN RELY ON ME — ER . . . I MEAN US!
COO . . . SMASHIN'! WIV OL' IRONSIDES UNDER MY CONTROL, I CAN MAKE 'IM DO ANYTHIN' I BLOOMIN' WELL LIKE!

AND SO, EARLY NEXT MORNING . . .
COME ON, TICH . . . BREAKFAST! AIN'T YOU COMIN' TO THE COOKHOUSE?
NOT ME, MATE! I'VE GOT OTHER PLANS THIS MORNIN'! HEH! HEH!
IRONSIDES! I WANT ME BREAKFAST IN BED . . . SO FETCH ME TWO BANGERS, FOUR RASHERS O' BACON, A FRIED EGG AN' A MUG O' CHAR! ON THE BLINKIN' DOUBLE! GOT THAT, RIVET-CHOPS?
YES, MAGG-OT!
BUT THE STEEL COMMANDO HADN'T BEEN TOLD EXACTLY WHERE TO GO . . . SO IT HEADED FOR THE NEAREST SOURCE OF FOOD! THE OFFICERS' MESS!
OFFICERS' MESS
KER-AASH!
I SAY, WHAT..?
GNAAAGH! MY BACON AND EGG! MY SAUSAGES! HURRICANE, WHAT THE DICKENS IS GOING ON?
SWIIIIPE!
SNATCH!
GRRR! I DON'T EXACTLY KNOW, COLONEL, BUT I'LL BET A YEAR'S FLIPPIN' PAY THAT MY BIRD-BRAINED BATMAN IS BEHIND IT ALL!
AND AS THE STEEL COMMANDO CLUMPED OFF . . . THE BIG MAN FOLLOWED!
AH, THANK YOU, MY GOOD MAN! JEST PLACE THE NOSH ON THIS 'ERE TRAY, THEN TROT OFF AN' TELL THE CAP'N THAT 'IS LORDSHIP MALONE WILL BE AVAILABLE FOR DUTY WITHIN THE 'OUR!
STAP ME SIDEWAYS! PERHAPS 'IS FLIPPIN' LORDSHIP WOULD LIKE TO TELL THE CAPTAIN IN PERSON! OR IS THAT ASKIN' TOO FLAMIN' MUCH FROM A HIGH-BORN BLISTERIN' BATMAN LIKE YOURSELF?
SO HELP ME, YOU DON'T KNOW IT YET, YOU MICKEY-TAKING SON OF A MINCE-FACED MEAT GRINDER, BUT THAT METAL MANIAC UNDER YOUR CONTROL HAS JUST WALKED IN AND WRECKED THE FLAMIN' OFFICERS' MESS!
WAAA-OOW! K-K-KEEP YER 'AIR ON, CAP'N, 'OW WUZ I TO KNOW 'E'D GO THERE INSTEAD O' THE BLINKIN' COOK'OUSE? I-I-I ONLY WANTED TO 'AVE BREAKFAST IN BED!
THIS IS THE BATTLE FOR BELGIUM, YOU BIRD-BRAIN, NOT A FIVE STAR HOTEL IN BLISTERING BRIGHTON! WHEN WE HIT THAT THUMPIN' OIL REFINERY I WANT YOU WIDE AWAKE, GOT IT?
GNUUUGH! A-AYE, AYE, CAP'N . I RECKON YOU'VE MADE YOUR POINT!
THWUMP!
AND LATER, THE MARINES SET OFF FOR THEIR OBJECTIVE — BUT AS THEY NEARED IT . . .
WELL, KEELHAUL ME IN A BARREL OF BLISTERING BRINY— THE KRAUTS HAVE GOT THIS PLACE SEWN UP AS TIGHT AS A MISER'S WALLET! MORTARS AND MACHINE GUNS EVERY FLIPPIN' WHERE!
WUMPFF!
KER-UMP!
FTOOM!
MOST OF THE FIRE IS COMING FROM THE VILLAGE, CAP'N! I SUGGEST MALONE AND THE STEEL COMMANDO LEAD THE ATTACK AND WINKLE THE JERRIES OUT HOUSE BY HOUSE!

FULL OF HIS OWN IMPORTANCE, MAGGOT STORMED FORWARD WITH THE MIGHTY ROBOT . . .
FASTER, METAL CHOPS, FASTER! FOR ONCE IN ME LIFE I'M GOIN' TO IMPRESS THAT BIG 'ULK 'URRICANE WIV ME ABILITY TO COMMAND!
THUMP!
BASH!
KAR-RUNCH!
YES, MAGG-OT!
KLUNK!
CRACK! CRACK!
THUKKA! THUKKA! THUKKA!
COMPLETELY CARRIED AWAY, THE LITTLE MAN BEGAN TO BARK ORDERS . . .
THAT'S IT, IRONSIDES! NOW SWING THOSE ARMS! KEEP YER 'EAD UP. . . UP! DIG THOSE HEELS IN, LAD . . . DIG 'EM IN, I SAID!
BIFF!
DONG!
ZUNK!
AT ONCE... MAGG-OT!
HEY! 'ANG ON! I DIDN'T MEAN LIKE THAT... OOOER!
CLUNG!
THWAAM!
CREE-AAAK!
KER-RAK!
BLISTER MY BILGES WITH A BENT BOAT HOOK, THE LAMB-BRAINED LITTLE LUGWORM HAS GONE AND SUNK HIMSELF IN A FLAMIN' CELLAR!
SOK!
MAGGOT WAS DAZED . . . BUT UNHURT!
S-SORRY ABAHT THIS LITTLE SLIP, CAP'N! BUT IRONSIDES MISUNDERSTOOD ME ORDERS AGAIN! 'AVE YOU GOT A ROPE TO HAUL US OUT?
NO I THUNDERIN' WELL HAVEN'T YOU DOZY-FACED DACE! USE THE FLIPPIN' CELLAR STAIRS!
MOMENTS LATER, AS MAGGOT AND THE STEEL COMMANDO REACHED THE SURFACE AGAIN . . .
RAT TAT TAT!
KRUMPP!
THE KRAUTS HAVE US ZEROED IN, SKIPPER! WE'LL NEVER ADVANCE THROUGH A CURTAIN OF FIRE LIKE THIS!
KA-WOOMPF!
SPAANG!
YOU'RE RIGHT, SHIPMATE! EVERYTHING DEPENDS ON THE STEEL COMMANDO!
HEAR THAT, IRONSIDES? IT'S ALL OR NOTHING NOW! SO PUT YOUR BEST FOOT FORWARD!
YES... MAGG-OT!
YAIEEEEEEE!
OH... NO! 'E PUT IS BEST FOOT FORWARD ALL RIGHT — STRAIGHT INTO THE SKIPPER'S STERN!
KATHOOMP!
BRR-UMPP!
YERSS... AN' HE'S GOIN' TO LAND ON TOP OF ONE OF THE OIL STORAGE TANKS!

THE LANDING WAS FAR FROM SOFT... AND THE NEXT MOMENT BELGIUM SEEMED TO BURST AT THE SEAMS AS THE COLOSSAL COMMANDO ERUPTED INTO ONE OF THE FIERCEST "RAGIN' FURIES" OF ALL TIME!
GREAT CREELS O' SALTED COD! I'M LUMBERED WITH THE MOST USELESS, FLEA-BRAINED, FLANNEL-FACED BATMAN AFLOAT! ALL HE HAS TO DO IS MAKE THAT THUNDERIN' TIN-MAN TOPPLE A FEW TEUTONS, AND WHAT HAPPENS? THAT RIVET-FACED ROBOT ENDS UP AS A CROSS BETWEEN A BUTLER, A COALMAN AND A FLAMIN' FOOTBALL STAR!
SEETHING WITH RAGE, HURRICANE SWARMED HALFWAY DOWN A FIXED METAL LADDER. AND THEN . . .
IRONSIDES ISN'T THE ONLY BLISTERING BLOKE WHO CAN PUT THE BOOT IN! NOW IT'S MY THUMPIN' TURN!
KER-LANG!
ZINK!
RAT-TAT TATTAT!
BLAM!
BELT ME BACKWARDS OVER BATTERSEA BRIDGE — IT'S A BLOOMIN' RIVER OF OIL!
GLUC-UC-CUC!
SWOOSH!
AYE, THE SKIPPER'S KICKED A HOLE IN THE TANK! THE SAUSAGE-NOSHERS WILL BE SWIMMIN' IN THAT STUFF IN A MINUTE!
DONNERWETTER!
SPAANG!
HIMMEL!
KRAK!
KRAK!
SURE ENOUGH, THE GERMANS WERE TAKEN COMPLETELY BY SURPRISE . . .
TEUFEL...DIS VOS LIKE DER GLUE! I CANNOT MOVE!
AAAGH!
SOK!
HA, HA! I'VE SENT THE STEEL COMMANDO IN TO MOP UP . . . BUT IF YOU ASK ME, 'E AIN'T NEEDED ANY MORE!
ZOK!
GLOOOP!
NEIN! GLAARRGH!
SLITHER!
MINUTES LATER, ALL RESISTANCE WAS AT AN END . . . AND MAGGOT GRINNED.
ONE OIL REFINERY TAKEN WIV NO CASUALTIES! THAT'S WOT I CALL A 'IGHLY SUCCESSFUL MISSION, CAP'N!
YES . . . BUT IT'S NO THANKS TO YOU, HALF-PINT! AND WHEN I GET BACK TO BASE, THERE'S SOMEONE I WANT TO VISIT!
AND, TWO DAYS LATER, IN THE UNIT SICK BAY . . .
THESE ARE FOR YOU, CORPORAL BATES! NOW PLEASE . . . PLEASE GET BETTER SOON, WON'T YOU?
WELL, IT'S VERY NICE OF YOU T'BE SO CONCERNED, CAP'N... BUT THE DOC WANTS ME TER STAY IN BED FOR AT LEAST ANOTHER FOUR DAYS!
FOUR DAYS! CAULK MY KEEL... I DON'T KNOW WHETHER I'LL HAVE THE FLIPPIN' STRENGTH TO LIVE THROUGH THEM! GROAN!
THANK YOU, MY MAN! NOW AFTER YOU'VE RUN MY BATH, WE'LL SEE ABOUT SOME LUNCH, ALL RIGHT?
YES... MAGG-OT!

FOR VALOUR

The Military Order

# of William

Major Tyler of the Irish Guards asked an American colleague if his GIs had ever crossed under enemy fire before.

"No," replied the cigar-chewing Colonel Tucker, "they're getting on-the-job training."

The British Major was appalled. Yet he also knew that these American troops had to cross the Waal River if their fellow parachutists of the British 1st Airborne Division, trapped near Arnhem, were to be rescued. The men of the US 82nd Airborne Division had not even seen canvas assault-boats before. Nor did they realise how wide the river was, and that there were a further eight hundred metres of open ground to cover even after they'd got across the water.

Shocked

When these Americans saw what they were up against they were shocked. It looked like a suicide mission. To make matters worse, their fragile boats had been delayed by an enemy air-raid some miles to the rear. They only arrived after the RAF had started to plaster the German defences across the Waal. From then on everything was chaos and confusion. The tiny boats each carried thirteen paratroopers and three crewmen to row. Hurriedly they were pushed into the river. Some got stuck. Some overturned. Others sank after being overloaded. A man kept yelling, "Keep going! Keep going!" Another officer prayed out loud, "Hail Mary — Full of Grace — Hail Mary — Full of Grace," to the beat of his little boat's wooden paddles.

The enemy's fire was heavy and accurate. Guns, mortars and artillery blew men and boats clean out of the water. For many minutes the Americans were completely exposed and unable to shoot back. At last some boats reached the far bank. Men got out and fired at their foes, then fell dead before they could take another step.

General Browning, commanding the British 1st Airborne Corps, watched the whole battle and said, "I have never seen a more gallant action." Browning was the man who had earlier warned Montgomery about the whole Arnhem operation, suggesting that the Allies might be "going a bridge too far".

Courage

Amid the carnage on the river some men had amazing escapes. Private Joseph Jedlicka fell from his boat and, loaded down with bandoliers of machine-gun bullets, sank like a stone. But he held his breath and just walked along the bottom until first his helmet and then his face appeared from the water on the far side of the river!

Despite all this courage, the Americans of the 504th, 505th and 508th Parachute Infantry Regiments could not advance far or fast enough to save their British comrades outside Arnhem. But their heroism wasn't forgotten. The units that took part and which spilt so much blood to liberate that little corner of Holland, were later awarded the Military Order of William. This is Holland's highest award for heroism. All surviving personnel were now allowed to wear the blue and orange lanyard of this proud Order.

The Military Order of William was created by King William I in 1815, two months before the battle of Waterloo in which the Dutch were, of course, Britain's allies. Its motto, "Voor Moed Beleid Trouw" (For Courage, Leadership and Loyalty) was certainly earned by those men who stormed across the river Waal on 20th September 1944.

With a resounding crash, the door of the garden shed flew open, and young Jim Frobisher's heart sank as the voice of his bullying guardian, Alf Hudson, sounded harshly in his ears . . .

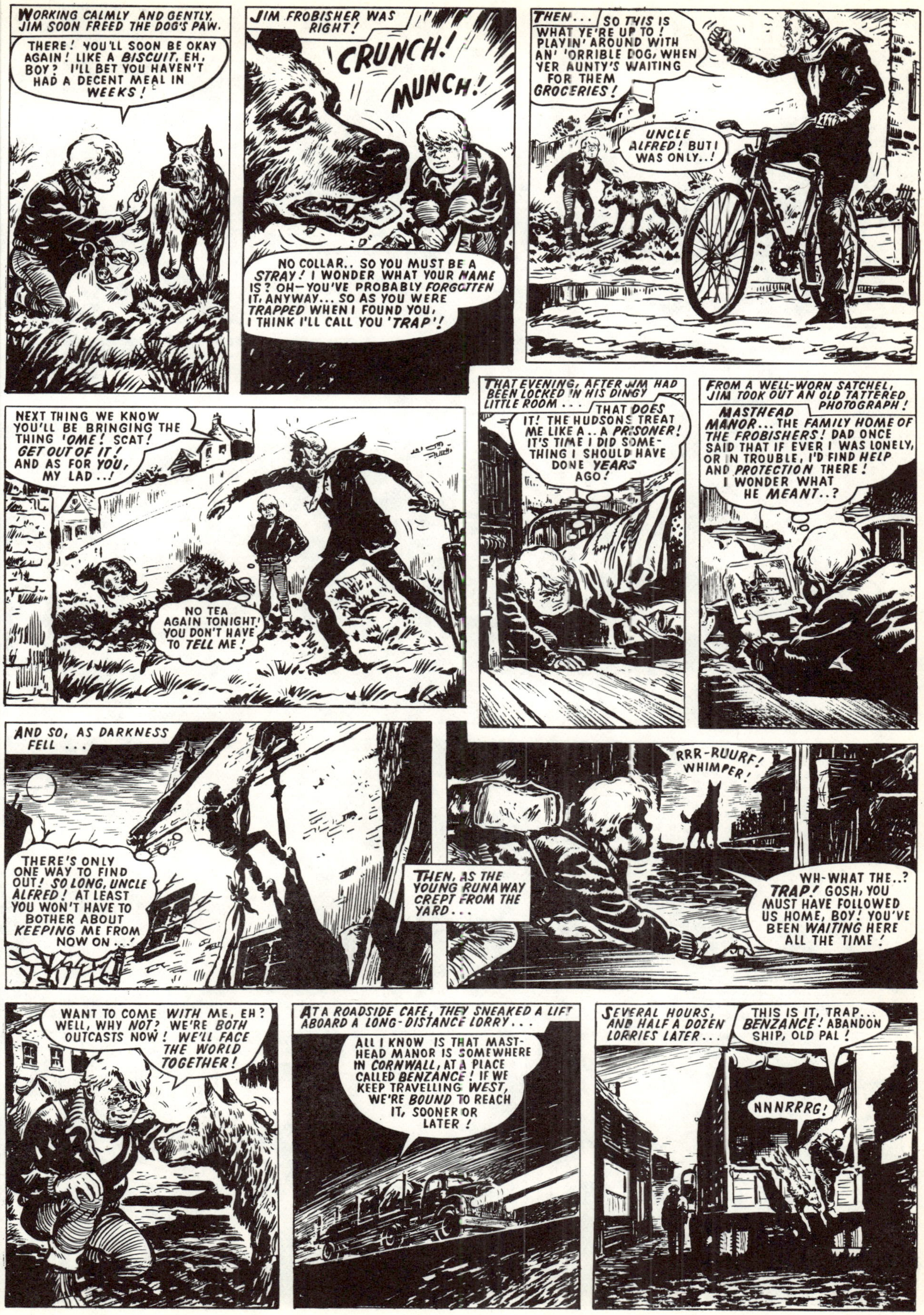
WORKING CALMLY AND GENTLY, JIM SOON FREED THE DOG'S PAW.
THERE! YOU'LL SOON BE OKAY AGAIN! LIKE A BISCUIT, EH, BOY? I'LL BET YOU HAVEN'T HAD A DECENT MEAL IN WEEKS!
JIM FROBISHER WAS RIGHT!
CRUNCH!
MUNCH!
NO COLLAR.. SO YOU MUST BE A STRAY! I WONDER WHAT YOUR NAME IS? OH—YOU'VE PROBABLY FORGOTTEN IT, ANYWAY... SO AS YOU WERE TRAPPED WHEN I FOUND YOU, I THINK I'LL CALL YOU 'TRAP'!
THEN...
SO THIS IS WHAT YE'RE UP TO! PLAYIN' AROUND WITH AN' 'ORRIBLE DOG, WHEN YER AUNTY'S WAITING FOR THEM GROCERIES!
UNCLE ALFRED! BUT I WAS ONLY..!
NEXT THING WE KNOW YOU'LL BE BRINGING THE THING 'OME! SCAT! GET OUT OF IT! AND AS FOR YOU, MY LAD..!
NO TEA AGAIN TONIGHT! YOU DON'T HAVE TO TELL ME!
THAT EVENING, AFTER JIM HAD BEEN LOCKED IN HIS DINGY LITTLE ROOM...
THAT DOES IT! THE HUDSONS TREAT ME LIKE A.. A PRISONER! IT'S TIME I DID SOMETHING I SHOULD HAVE DONE YEARS AGO!
FROM A WELL-WORN SATCHEL, JIM TOOK OUT AN OLD TATTERED PHOTOGRAPH!
MASTHEAD MANOR... THE FAMILY HOME OF THE FROBISHERS! DAD ONCE SAID THAT IF EVER I WAS LONELY, OR IN TROUBLE, I'D FIND HELP AND PROTECTION THERE! I WONDER WHAT HE MEANT..?
AND SO, AS DARKNESS FELL...
THERE'S ONLY ONE WAY TO FIND OUT! SO LONG, UNCLE ALFRED! AT LEAST YOU WON'T HAVE TO BOTHER ABOUT KEEPING ME FROM NOW ON...!
THEN, AS THE YOUNG RUNAWAY CREPT FROM THE YARD...
RRR-RUURF! WHIMPER!
WH-WHAT THE..? TRAP! GOSH, YOU MUST HAVE FOLLOWED US HOME, BOY! YOU'VE BEEN WAITING HERE ALL THE TIME!
WANT TO COME WITH ME, EH? WELL, WHY NOT? WE'RE BOTH OUTCASTS NOW! WE'LL FACE THE WORLD TOGETHER!
AT A ROADSIDE CAFE, THEY SNEAKED A LIFT ABOARD A LONG-DISTANCE LORRY...
ALL I KNOW IS THAT MASTHEAD MANOR IS SOMEWHERE IN CORNWALL, AT A PLACE CALLED BENZANCE! IF WE KEEP TRAVELLING WEST, WE'RE BOUND TO REACH IT, SOONER OR LATER!
SEVERAL HOURS, AND HALF A DOZEN LORRIES LATER...
THIS IS IT, TRAP... BENZANCE! ABANDON SHIP, OLD PAL!
NNNRRRG!

WITH THE TANG OF THE SEA IN THEIR NOSTRILS, BOY AND DOG SLIPPED THROUGH THE DESERTED FISHING VILLAGE!
MASTHEAD POINT... WHICH MEANS THE MANOR MUST BE UP THIS WAY, SOMEWHERE! COME ON..!
THEN A NAGGING DOUBT BEGAN TO GROW IN JIM FROBISHER'S MIND!
THE MANOR MUST HAVE BEEN UNOCCUPIED FOR YEARS, TRAP! SUPPOSE SOMEONE'S BOUGHT IT, OR... OR IT'S BEEN PULLED DOWN? WE'LL HAVE COME ALL THIS WAY FOR NOTHING!
BUT AS THEY CLIMBED A FLINTY WALL, AND EMERGED AGAIN INTO THE MOONLIGHT...
NO, TRAP... IT'S STILL THERE! MASTHEAD MANOR! WE'RE HOME!
WAAAF!
NOT UNTIL HE HAD LED THE WAY UP A FLIGHT OF CREAKING STEPS, AND INTO THE DANK SHADOWS OF THE STRANGE OLD HOUSE, DID JIM FROBISHER REALISE WHY MASTHEAD MANOR WAS STILL THERE!
GOSH! IT'S BECOME SUCH A SHAMBLES, NO-ONE IN HIS RIGHT MIND WOULD WANT TO LIVE HERE! BUT WE'RE GOING TO, TRAP! WE'LL HAVE THE WHOLE PLACE TO OURSELVES..!
EVEN AS JIM SPOKE...
SLURSH-CLONK!
SLURSH-CLONK!
SLURSH-CLONK!
GRRR-RRRRG!
MY STARS... F-FOOTSTEPS! ECHOING THROUGH THE HOUSE! THEY'RE COMING... CLOSER..!
AND THEN...
DON'T MOVE ANOTHER STEP!
BEFORE JIM FROBISHER'S ASTONISHED EYES... A ROARING, GLOWING SHAPE BEGAN TO SQUEEZE THROUGH THE PORTHOLE...
WHO GAVE YE PERMISSION TO COME ABOARD THE MANOR?
BAAA-OOOM!
CLANGA-LANG!

AVAST THERE, YE SCURVY, KNOCK-KNEED LANDLUBBERS! 'TIS ONLY DOOM AND DESTRUCTION YE'LL FIND ABOARD THE MANOR! ACTION STATIONS! PREPARE TO REPEL BOARDERS!
OH, M-MY STARS..!
EVEN THE PLUCKY YOUNG RUNAWAY WAS UNNERVED BY THE BELLOWING APPARITION!
HA-HAAAR! RUN, YE MANGY SONS OF SEA-COOKS...!
IT'S A GHOST, TRAP! YOU CAN S-SEE RIGHT THROUGH IT! LET'S GET OUT OF HERE!
THE ROARING, WILD-EYED FIGURE FLUNG OUT AN ARM...
..BUT THERE BE NO ESCAPE FROM THE GUARDIAN OF MASTHEAD MANOR!
WAAAAHH!
YE'LL SUFFER THE SAME FATE AS EVERY CHEEKY MAN-JACK WHO'S DARED TO SET FOOT IN THE LAST STRONGHOLD OF THE FROBISHERS!
THAT CUTLASS! IT'S.. FLOATING DOWN FROM THE WALL! COMING AT ME...!
IN THE NICK OF TIME, JIM FROBISHER LEAPT ASIDE!
AAAOWWW!
MISSED, BY THUNDER! BUT THE NEXT BLOW WILL CLEAVE HIS TOPSAILS...!
THEN...
RRROWWRL!
NO, TRAP! GET BACK... KEEP AWAY FROM IT! YOU CAN'T DO ANY HARM TO A GHOST!
WAF!
WAF!
BUT JIM FROBISHER WAS WRONG!
AAAAARG! SCAT! HAUL 'IM OFF! 'E BE ARTER ME WOODEN LEG!
GNAARG!
SNAP!
PERHAPS IT WAS THE ECHOING HOWLS OF THE PRANCING SPECTRE WHICH DISTURBED THE RUBBISH, PILED HIGH IN THE DUSTY HALL. FOR, SUDDENLY...
KREE-EEEEEK!
UUUHHH?
TRAP, LOOK OUT! ALL THAT STUFF IS STARTING TO TOPPLE...!
YEEEAAARG!
CRAAASH!
BOM!
CLOINNNG!
ZONNNK!
WELL, CLAP ME IN IRONS! GROAN! THAT TREACHEROUS LEG-SNAPPIN' CUR 'AS RUINED ME PERFORMANCE!

BUT THE BATTLE AIN'T FINISHED YET, BY GLORY! I'LL CALL ON ALL ME GHASTLY POWERS TO WREAK A HIDEOUS VENGEANCE!
HEE, HEE, OH, MY GOSH! HA, HA, HAAAA!
THE GHOST OF MASTHEAD MANOR PAUSED IN AMAZEMENT!
BY THE TRADES OF JAVA! SILENCE, YE SAUCY WHELP! NO-ONE LAUGHS AT FIREBRAND FROBISHER!
I.. C-CAN'T HELP IT! HAH, HAH! IT WAS YOUR HEAD, STICKING OUT FROM THAT BARREL! IT... L-LOOKED SO FUNNY!
BAAA-OOOOM!
GAAAAH! MAYBE YE WON'T FIND IT SO RIB-TICKLING WHEN YOUR OWN HEAD IS ROLLING IN THE DUST!
RATTLE!
WOO-EEEEEEEE!
IT'S NO USE! YOU JUST DON'T FRIGHTEN ME ANYMORE! ALL THE CRASHING AND BANGING AND ROARING IN THE WORLD WON'T SCARE ME AWAY NOW!
BESIDES, I'VE GOT EVERY RIGHT TO BE RIGHT! MY NAME'S JIM FROBISHER, AND AS FAR AS I KNOW, MASTHEAD MANOR STILL BELONGS TO MY FAMILY! IT'S GOING TO BE MY HOME FROM NOW ON!
YOU? A...A FROBISHER?
ALTHOUGH HE COULD HARDLY BELIEVE IT WAS ALL HAPPENING, JIM FOUND HIMSELF EXPLAINING THE WHOLE STORY... TO A GHOST!
...SO HERE I AM, AND HERE I'M GOING TO STAY! IF DAD IS STILL ALIVE, HE'LL GET IN TOUCH WITH ME ONE DAY! I KNOW HE WILL!
BY THE BEARD OF DAVY JONES! SO YOU ARE OLD BEN FROBISHER'S BOY..!
AND HERE AM I, TRYING TO HAUNT ONE OF ME OWN RELATIVES! IT'S AS WELL THAT DOG O' YOURN HAD A GO AT FIREBRAND FROBISHER!
GOSH! THEN YOU MUST BE ONE OF MY ANCESTORS!
AYE, LAD! YOU'RE GAZIN' AT PERHAPS THE GREATEST FROBISHER OF THEM ALL! THE FINEST SKIPPER THAT EVER SAILED A THREE-MASTER ON A PORT TACK, WITH THE WIND SINGING IN HER WEATHER-BRACES!
YOU LOOK MORE LIKE A PIRATE TO ME, MR. FIREBRAND.. OR PERHAPS A SMUGGLER!
I BEEN MOST THINGS IN MY TIME, JIM, LAD! THE MANOR HAS BEEN MY HOME, TOO, FOR NIGH ON THREE HUNDRED YEARS! SO WHAT SAY WE THROW IN OUR LOT, AND SAIL 'ER TOGETHER? ME AN' YOU, AND THAT BLISTERIN,' LEG-GNAWING HOUND!
AYE, THAT'S IT, BY THUNDER! WE'LL DEFEND THE MANOR AGAINST ANY CREW O' LANDLUBBERS THAT TRY TO TAKE IT FROM US! FOLLOW ME, BOY... TOPSIDE!
FIREBRAND, WAIT A MINUTE! YOU'RE FORGETTING THAT I CAN'T WALK THROUGH WALLS!

SOMEHOW, JIM AND TRAP FOUND THEIR WAY ON TO THE ROOF!
MR. FIRE-BRAND, WHERE ARE YOU?
UP 'ERE, SHIPMATE... IN THE CROW'S NEST!
OLD FIREBRAND AIN'T HAD MUCH CAUSE TO CELEBRATE SINCE YER POOR FATHER WEIGHED ANCHOR, BUT I RECKON THIS BE TIME TO HOIST THE FLAG OF THE FROBISHERS AGAIN..!
THE FIGHTING FROBISHERS
AND THERE SHE BLOWS! HA-HAAAAR!
IN A FLASH, THE GHOST OF FIREBRAND FROBISHER RE-JOINED THE OTHER TWO MEMBERS OF THE STRANGEST FAMILY IN THE WORLD!
SO LET'S SWEAR AN OATH ON IT, ME HEARTIES... NEVER TO DESERT THE HOME OF THE FROBISHERS, SO LONG AS 'ER BATTLE-COLOURS BE FLYIN' FROM THE MAST-HEAD!
YOU SAID IT, FIREBRAND!
GRRR-AFF!
THE NEXT MORNING...
SNAAWWW-FUU-UUURGH!
M-MY GOSH... LISTEN, TRAP! WHAT ON EARTH CAN BE MAKING THAT GHASTLY, GROANING NOISE?
GRRRRRR!
FNUUUURG-HOOOOOO!
IT SEEMS TO BE COMING FROM THE GALLEY...I-I MEAN, THE KITCHEN! DON'T SAY THAT MASTHEAD MANOR IS HAUNTED BY TWO GHOSTS!
BUT AS THE ALARMED JIM EDGED CAUTIOUSLY INTO THE KITCHEN...
SNAAAAW-GUUURFLE!
TH-THANK THE STARS... IT'S ALL RIGHT, TRAP! IT'S ONLY OLD FIREBRAND, SNORING HIS GHOSTLY HEAD OFF!
I RECKON IT'S TIME WE GAVE HIM A SCARE! HEE, HEEE! WATCH WHAT HAPPENS WHEN I WHIP THE HAMMOCK AWAY FROM UNDER HIM..!

THWAAAP!
... LIKE THAT! WHOOPEEEEE! FALL AWAY, FIREBRAND!
BUT TO JIM'S UTTER AMAZEMENT...
THE HAMMOCK WAS ONLY FOR SHOW, JIM, LAD! WE SPIRITS CAN FLOAT LIKE ALBATROSSES ON THE WIND! HA, HA, HAAAAAAA!
DARN IT! I SHOULD HAVE THOUGHT OF THAT!
YOU'LL SOON GET USED TO BERTHIN' WITH A GHOST, ME HEARTY! BUT HOW DOES IT FEEL, ON THIS FINE MORNING, TO BE MASTER OF MASTHEAD MANOR?
GREAT! IF IT WASN'T FOR THE FACT THAT TRAP AND I ARE STARVING!
YOU LET OLD FIREBRAND WORRY ABOUT THAT! TACK ALONG TO THE DININ' ROOM, AND I'LL BE THERE IN A JIFF WITH A FEAST FIT FOR A CAPTAIN'S TABLE!
BLIP!
AND, SURE ENOUGH, MOMENTS LATER...
HOW'S THAT THEN, SHIPMATE..? WITH THE COMPLIMENTS OF ME SPIRIT FRIENDS! CHEESE, SALT PORK, SHIP'S BISCUIT, AND A TANKARD OF FINE MEAD!
COR!
BUT, AS JIM SAT DOWN AND REACHED EAGERLY FOR A CHUNK OF CHEESE...
UUUUHH? YOU CHUMP, FIREBRAND! THIS STUFF ISN'T ANY GOOD TO ME! IT'S GHOST FOOD! MY HAND WENT CLEAN THROUGH IT!
THUNDERIN' BROADSIDES! SO IT DID!
NEVER MIND! AT LEAST YOU TRIED! IT'S ABOUT TIME I STARTED LEARNING TO FEND FOR MYSELF, ANYWAY!
HOLD ON THERE, JIM...!

Continue this thrilling picture-story on page 85

FOR VALOUR

Congressional

As the fog cleared from the battlefield, Sergeant John Latham saw that he and his men were alone. They had staggered forward through the smoke-screen amid devastating enemy fire that came from every direction at once. Somehow John Latham's little platoon from the US Army's 107th Machine Gun Company advanced further into the Germans' carefully planned Hindenburg Line defences than any of their comrades. So now they were alone — except for the Kaiser's troops who seemed to be all around. The date was September 29th, 1918, and the First World War would soon be over. At the moment, however, the German Army still had plenty of fight left.

Suddenly Sergeant Latham saw, through his binoculars, a friendly uniform. An American officer was trying to catch the attention of the machine-gun platoon. Near him was an American tank, but unfortunately it had not come to help Latham's men. Instead the tank was disabled and stuck. Its commander wanted the machine-gunners to rescue him and his crew!

Already the Germans were throwing everything they had at the trapped American tank, including mortar-bombs, machine-gun and rifle fire. Sergeant Latham called on Sergeant Eggers and Corporal O'Shea to follow him, and dashed through the enemy barrage. Almost at once O'Shea was killed. He was carrying their only machine-gun and that was also smashed. Now they were virtually unarmed, but Latham and Eggers pressed on until at last they reached the tank.

Scrambling inside, they grabbed one of the tank's machine-guns. The officer and two of his men were still alive, but all were wounded. Now Latham and Eggers were also hit, though not seriously. Miraculously these five wounded men managed to crawl back to the safety of a shell-hole. Desperately, Sergeant Latham mounted his new gun on the edge of the crater — only just in time. At that moment a German detachment attacked but were turned back by Latham's fire.

Still the Americans' ordeal wasn't over, for when Sergeant Eggers and two other injured men tried to go for help they soon got trapped in another, smaller, shell-hole. Only when night fell were Sergeants Latham and Eggers able to lead their small group of sixteen survivors, eleven of whom were wounded, back to the Allied lines.

Not surprisingly John Latham and Alan Eggers were awarded the Congressional Medal of Honor, as was Corporal Thomas O'Shea. The three men also received medals from Britain, France, Italy, Portugal and even Montenegro.

The Congressional Medal of Honor is America's highest decoration for gallantry. The Navy version was authorised in 1861, while that for the Army was started a year later. Today there is also a Medal of Honor for the Air Force and even a Space Medal of Honor, which is the

Medal of Honor

decoration for astronauts.

Some confusion arose towards the end of the last century when various veterans' organisations started to wear medals that looked like the Congressional Medal of Honor. In 1904 a new version was designed and was then patented by the US Secretary for War so that nobody could copy it again. In 1916 the Government went even further to protect this award by setting up a board of enquiry to study all the Army versions that had been given so far. Eventually they struck over nine hundred names from the list and ordered any who were still alive to give their medals back! Unfortunately this included Dr. Mary Walker, the only woman to be given a Congressional Medal of Honor.

CAPTAIN HURRICANE
ONCE WE GET THIS FLIPPIN' LOAD OF SUPPLIES TO OUR LADS, WE'LL BE READY TO MOVE AGAINST THOSE SLANT-EYED RICE-NOSHERS! IT'S ABOUT TIME WE— MALONE! ARE YOU FLAMIN' WELL LISTENIN' TO ME?
EH..? UHH— WASSAT, CAP'N?
IN 1944, THE BRITISH FOURTEENTH ARMY UNDER GENERAL SLIM WAS BEGINNING TO TURN THE TIDE AGAINST THE JAPANESE INVADERS OF BURMA. AMONG THE TROOPS SUPPORTING THE ADVANCING BRITISH WAS CAPTAIN HERCULES HURRICANE AND HIS UNIT OF ROYAL MARINE COMMANDOS. ONE AFTERNOON, IN A TRUCK WITH HIS PINT-SIZED BATMAN, MAGGOT MALONE...
MALONE SUDDENLY AWOKE FROM HIS DAYDREAM...
OOP! SORRY, CAP'N! I WAS THINKIN'! THERE'S SOMETHIN' I FORGOT! I TIED A KNOT IN ME 'ANKY, SEE, AN'..!
NEVER MIND THAT, YOU LAMB-BRAINED LUGWORM— WATCH WHERE YOU'RE BLUNDERIN' WELL DRIVIN'! YOU'LL HAVE US IN THE..!
THE TRUCK SHOT FORWARD—AND NOSE-DIVED INTO THE RIVER!
GAAH! BLISTERIN' BARNACLES! ARE YOU TRYIN' TO PERISHIN' WELL SCUPPER ME, YOU PEANUT-BRAINED PERIWINKLE?
COR— I'M SORRY, CAP'N! ME 'AND SORTA SLIPPED!
SPER-LOSSH!
WELL—YOU'VE REALLY GOT US IN A THUMPIN' MESS THIS TIME, SHRIMP! YOU'D BETTER SLIP BACK TO BASE AND FETCH THE BREAK-DOWN TRUCK! YOU CAN GO UP-RIVER IN THAT INFLATABLE DINGHY!
LUMME— IT'S ABOUT TEN BLOOMIN' MILES!
SO MAGGOT SET OFF, PADDLING BACK TO BASE. BUT HE WAS BEING WATCHED...
OL' FATHER THAMES KEEPS ROLLIN' ALONG!
BY SHINTO! IT IS A SMALL ENGLISH PIG! THERE MUST BE MORE OF THEM NEARBY!
WE MUST WARN HEAD-QUARTERS!
THE LITTLE MAN REACHED BASE SAFELY—BUT...
I'VE GOT NO DRIVERS TO SPARE! YOU CAN TAKE THIS BREAKDOWN TRUCK, BUT YOU'LL HAVE TO DRIVE IT YOURSELF!
'SALL RIGHT, SARGE! I'M A DAB-'AND WITH ONE OF THEM!
MAGGOT HADN'T GONE FAR WHEN HE HEARD A STRANGE NOISE!
WHOOOOOO!
'ELLO— WHAT'S THAT BLOOMIN' MOANIN' SOUND? IT'S COMIN' FROM THAT THERE 'OLE OVER THERE! I'D BETTER JUST 'AVE A QUICK DEKKO!

THEN, TO THE LITTLE BATMAN'S SURPRISE...
AAAH! LOOK AT THAT! A LITTLE ELEPHANT WHAT'S GOT TRAPPED IN A BLINKIN' GREAT 'OLE! 'ANG ON, MATE! I'LL SOON 'AVE YOU OUT OF IT!
WHOODDD!
MAGGOT BACKED THE TRUCK ON TO THE HOLE, AND WINCHED UP THE BABY ELEPHANT!
THAT'S IT, MATEY! HANG ON WITH YER TRUNK! YOU'LL BE UP THE BLINKIN' TOP IN A COUPLE OF SHAKES!
THERE Y'ARE, JUMBO! YOU'LL BE ALL RIGHT NOW! 'OP OFF BACK TO YER MUM, BEFORE YOU GET INTO MORE TROUBLE!
WHOOUP!
WHEN THE BABY ELEPHANT HAD GONE, MAGGOT DROVE ON TO MEET HIS SKIPPER...
MALONE—YOU LEAD-SWINGIN' LUBBER! WHERE IN HECK HAVE YOU BEEN ALL THIS TIME?
OH—JUST 'ELPIN' A FRIEND OUT OF A BIT OF A 'OLE, CAP'N!
THE WINCH WAS HITCHED TO THE TRUCK, BUT ALTHOUGH MAGGOT RAN THE WINDING MECHANISM AT FULL POWER, IT WOULD NOT PULL FREE—THEN...
GIVE IT FULL THROTTLE, TICH—NOW!
IT'S ON FULL POWER, CAP'N! IT JUST WON'T SHIFT! 'ERE—WHAT'S THAT TICKLIN' ME?
THE TWO COMMANDOS SWUNG ROUND...
WHAT THE BLUE PURPLE BLAZES ARE THOSE HULKIN' BRUTES DOIN' HERE?
PH-WEE-UPP!
OINNPH!
LUMME—IT'S ME OLD MATE JUMBO—AND 'E'S BROUGHT 'IS MUM, TOO! 'ANG ON A BIT, CAP'N! THESE ELEPHANTS GIVE ME AN IDEA!
MAGGOT MANAGED TO MAKE THE ELEPHANTS UNDERSTAND. THEN...
OOOMPH!
THAT'S IT, FELLERS! GRAB TIGHT 'OLD — AND PULL! SHE'S COMIN', CAP'N!
YOU'RE FLAMIN' WELL RIGHT, TICH! THANKS TO YOUR MATES, HERE!
SOON, THE TRUCK WAS OUT OF THE WATER...
THE FRONT WHEELS ARE BUCKLED, TICH! WE'LL HAVE TO PUT ON THE SPARES! TAKE HER UP, WILL YOU?
RIGHTO, CAP'N! UP SHE GOES—HUP!

UNFORTUNATELY, THE BIG ELEPHANT UNDERSTOOD THE WORD "HUP" DIFFERENTLY..!
THAT'S IT, TICH! NOW IF YOU— WHEAAAGH! WHAT'S HAPPENING? TELL THIS PERISHIN' ANIMAL TO PUT ME DOWN!
OO-ER! JUMBO'S MUM MUST UNDERSTAND ENGLISH! PUT 'IM DOWN, NOW! PUT 'IM DOWN, THERE'S A GOOD GIRL!
THE ELEPHANT HEARD MAGGOT'S WORDS, AND DROPPED HURRICANE— INTO THE RIVER!
L-LUMME— THAT'S DONE IT! SHE'S DROPPED 'IM THE BLOOMIN' DRINK!
SPLAASH!
HOINNGGG?
FURIOUS, THE MIGHTY MARINE SPLASHED OUT OF THE WATER, UNAWARE THAT HIS MOVEMENTS WERE BEING WATCHED BY A PARTY OF JAPS!
HOWLIN' HORNPIPES! GET THOSE THUMPIN' ANIMALS OUT OF HERE, MALONE, BEFORE I LOSE MY FLIPPIN' TEMPER!
AH, SO! BIG STUPID ENGLISH PIG DOES NOT SEE US! WE WILL ATTACK THEM, COMRADES! WAIT FOR MY COMMAND!
OUT OF THE WATER, THE MIGHTY MARINE CHANGED THE FRONT WHEELS. THEN...
THAT'S GOT THE FLIPPIN' THINGS ON, TICH! YOU CAN LET THE FRONT END DOWN NOW!
AYE, AYE, CAP'N! DOWN SHE GOES!
WAIT FOR WORD, COMRADES!
MAGGOT DID AS HE WAS TOLD! BUT...
YEEOOOWWW!
READY! FIRE!
COO— WHAT 'APPENED, CAP'N?
KR-AASH!
THE JAPS OPENED FIRE WITH GRENADES AND MACHINE GUNS...
SEE, COMRADES! WE HAVE SCORED DIRECT HIT! ENGLISH PIGS' TRUCK IS BROKEN!
WATCH OUT, CAP'N!
BLAAM!
RAT-TAT-TAT-TAT!
THE CRANE JIB BROKE OFF, AND FELL— STRAIGHT ON TOP OF THE GIANT CAPTAIN!
ZONKK!
RAT-TAT-TAT-TAT!
WHUUMP!
YEEAARRGHHH!
FORWARD, COMRADES! BANZAI! BANZAI!
AS THE JAPANESE REACHED THE OTHER SIDE OF THE RIVER, THEY STARED IN ASTONISHMENT AS THE MIGHTY MARINE ROARED TO HIS FEET, HIS ENORMOUS FRAME VIBRATING UNDER THE POWER OF A TREMENDOUS "RAGIN' FURY"!
THUNDERIN' TORNADOES! THAT JUST ABOUT TAKES THE THUMPIN' SHIP'S BISCUIT! I'M A MILD-MANNERED MOUSE OF A MAN, BUT AFTER I'VE BEEN DUNKED IN THE RIVER BY A FLAMIN' ELEPHANT, HAD A TRUCK DROPPED ON ME FLIPPIN' FOOT BY ME BIRD-BRAINED BATMAN, I'M CLONKED ON THE BONCE BY A CHUNK OF A PERISHIN' CRANE! WELL, NOW I'VE LOST MY TEMPER, AND THOSE JAPS ARE GOIN' TO BLISTERIN' WELL SUFFER!

PICKING UP THE HEAVY CRANE JIB, THE GIANT CAPTAIN BELTED INTO THE JAPS AS THEY STEPPED OFF THEIR RAFTS...
SCRAPE MY BILGES! TRY TO TAKE THE RISE OUT OF ME, WOULD YOU, YOU SNEAKY, WALL-EYED, DAFFODIL-COLOURED DUMMIES? WELL, I'LL TEACH YOU SOME THUMPIN' MANNERS!
OOWW!
KLAANG!
BONG!
BY SHINTO!
ZONGG!
HELP! THE WHITE GIANT HAS GONE MAD!
MEANWHILE, HURRICANE'S YELLS HAD FLOATED ACROSS THE JUNGLE, TO WHERE A HERD OF ELEPHANTS WERE GRAZING. THOSE BELLOWS MEANT SOMETHING TO THE BIG BULL ELEPHANT, THE LEADER OF THE HERD...
YEEOOOOWW! YEAAAARCH!
EOOOINNGG!
THE BULL GAVE A TREMENDOUS BELLOW, AND CRASHED FORWARD, FOLLOWED BY THE OTHERS...
HAAOINNGG!
CRASH!
CRAASH!
MEANWHILE, THE COLOSSAL COMMANDO WAS JUST FINISHING...
COOL OFF IN THERE, YOU FLAMIN' PIANO-TOOTHED WEEVILS!
BANZAI!
BANZAI!
BANZAI!
CAP'N! LOOK OUT! THERE'S MORE OF 'EM COMIN'! A WHOLE BLINKIN' ARMY THIS TIME!
THEN SUDDENLY, FROM OUT OF THE JUNGLE BURST THE ELEPHANT HERD!
HEOINGG!
HEWAAHH!
CRUMBS, CAP'N! LOOK—IT'S JUMBO AND 'IS MATES!
CRASH!
CRAASH!
BY THE BEARD OF MY ANCESTORS! LOOK WHAT COMES!
FLEE, COMRADES, FLEE!
THE ELEPHANTS CHARGED INTO THE RIVER— AND THE JAPS FLED IN A PANIC!
EEARGHH!
HEWAAHH!
GEWAAH!
KER-AASH!
BY SHINTO! WE ARE LOST!
SMAASH!
YOUUUWW! HELP!
WITH THE JAPS UTTERLY ROUTED, ONE LITTLE ELEPHANT REMAINED BEHIND...
THANKS FOR YER 'ELP, JUMBO MATE! COO— YOU 'AVE GOT A LONG NOSE, AIN'T YER? AND I REMEMBER NOW WHAT I'D FORGOT ABOUT, CAP'N! YER AUNT 'ARRIET SENT YOU A BIG BOX OF 'ANKERCHIEFS!
THANKS, TICH! WHEN WE GET BACK, YOU PACK 'EM WITH ME OTHERS IN MY BIG TRUNK! HA! HA!

FOR VALOUR

The Military Order

It was rare for air-aces to meet in combat, but it did happen sometimes. Lieutenant-Commander Banfield of the Austrian Navy and Lieutenant Baracca of the Italian Army fought in January 1917 and their combat was particularly unusual because the Austrian was flying a fighter flying-boat and the Italian a standard First World War biplane.

Both men were also exceptional. Gottfried Banfield had been a pilot since before the War broke out, as had Francesco Baracca. Banfield flew in the Imperial Naval Air Force's first operations against the Montenegro coast while Baracca took part in the Italian Army Air Force's first air-to-air combat. Although he was still a junior officer, the Italian was an ace with six kills to his credit. Banfield, however, was a senior officer in command of the Adriatic naval air station at Trieste. He had already downed four enemy aircraft and four observation balloons.

Nearly froze

On that bitter day when Banfield and Baracca met in January 1917, the icy Bora wind was blowing hard. The two pilots nearly froze in their open cockpits as they twisted and turned over the Isonzo river. To the north the Alps lay under a mantle of snow while to the south the Adriatic sparkled in a low winter sun. Below them the Austro-Italian Front had lain quiet since Italy's ninth bloody attempt to break through her enemy's defences. Several more months would pass before yet another unsuccessful push would be made in the Tenth Battle of the Isonzo.

Greater speed

Meanwhile, high above, the aerial combat was just as inconclusive. Neither Banfield nor Baracca could seize an advantage although the Austrian did notice that the clean lines and powerful 150 hp Benz engine of his "star-strutter" KDW flying-boat gave him greater speed than his opponent's manoeuverable little Nieuport 11.

Famous award

By the end of the war Gottfried Banfield had achieved nine confirmed victories, although Baracca had already died with thirty-four to his credit. None the less Banfield's contribution to the morale of the Austro-Hungarian Navy was so great that in March 1918 he was made a Knight of the Maria Theresa Military Order. This was one of Europe's first and most famous awards for gallantry. His old Lohner Type L flying-boat of 1914 was also taken around the Empire on display.

Warlike Empress

The ancient Hapsburg Empire of Austria-Hungary that Lieutenant-Commander Banfield had served faithfully throughout the war, ceased to exist in 1918. One of its rulers, the warlike Empress Maria Theresa, created the Military Order in her own name in 1757 after the great battle of Kolin. Like so many such medals, the Military Order of Maria Theresa came in three classes. The first grade, which Banfield won, was that of the Knight. Next came the Commander, and finally there was the Grand Cross of the Order which could be won only by outstandingly successful generals.

Democratic

The famous award of the Military Order of Maria Theresa, despite being created in one of the harshest empires in Europe, was surprisingly democratic for the 18th century. Maria Theresa's Order could be given to any soldier who showed particular bravery in the face of the enemy. His rank, his race and his religion were ignored, and such heroes not only got large pensions but were also raised into the ranks of the hereditary nobility. Although not surprisingly the Military Order of Maria Theresa was very *difficult* to win. In its one hundred and eighty years of war-torn history, this medal was given only 1,240 times.

The aerial combat was just as inconclusive. The icy Bora wind was blowing hard.

# of Maria Theresa

Wembley

THE F.A. Cup Final has a special magic no other domestic competition can match.

It's an occasion greater than any club or individual player, it is also a day that not only belongs to this nation, for thanks to TV the F.A. Cup Final is now watched by an estimated 500 million throughout the world. It's a day when reputations are won and lost, a day when past glories count for nothing — a day when heroes are born.

The F.A. Cup was instituted in the 1871-72 season when 15 clubs, all amateurs, entered.

They included Queen's Park from Scotland, but although the Scots reached the Semi-Finals they scratched because they could not afford to travel to London.

The first F.A. Cup winners were the Wanderers who beat Royal Engineers 1-0 at Kennington Oval (now the home of Surrey County Cricket) before a crowd of around 2,000 people.

The Oval continued to be the home of the Final until 1892 when the F.A. decided to take the game elsewhere because of the ever increasing interest in the Final.

Eventually, in 1923, history was made when the magnificent new Wembley Stadium staged one of the most memorable Finals of all time.

More than 250,000 fans besieged Wembley to watch Bolton Wanderers and West Ham United, many of whom never saw a ball kicked in the game that caused a sensation.

Bolton, who beat West Ham 2-0, were F.A. Cup winners three times during the first seven years of the Wembley Final.

In 1952 Newcastle United became the first club to win the trophy in two successive seasons at Wembley, but Tottenham Hotspur repeated this magnificent feat with victories in 1961 and 1962.

The men from White Hart Lane achieved a stupendous performance when they became the first club ever to record a "double double" when they beat Manchester City in 1981, after a replay in the 100th F.A. Cup Final, and retained the trophy in 1981-82 after two dramatic games against Queens Park Rangers.

WEMBLEY FACTS

45,000 of Wembley's 100,000 capacity are seated. The attendance is limited to 92,000 for evening floodlit games.

1,500 police officers control a Cup Final crowd for which there are 500 commissionaires, 500 honorary F.A. stewards and 100 first aid attendants on duty. 80 car park officials supervise 5,000 cars and 500 coaches.

A catering staff of 500 serve 400 lunches for officials and guests as well as operate 14 buffet bars. 25,000 sandwiches, 20,000 cups of tea, 60,000 bottles of beer and 500 bottles of whisky are consumed on Cup Final day.

CUP FINAL ODDITIES

The 1981-82 F.A. Cup Final between Spurs and Q.P.R. was the 101st and 54th to be staged at Wembley. Tottenham won the replay to equal Aston Villa's record of seven successes.

Tottenham were the first team to achieve the F.A. Cup and League double this century. They did it in 1961 and Arsenal emulated their feat in 1971. Preston North End in 1889 and Aston Villa in 1897 had been the first two clubs to achieve it.

The first team to appear in three consecutive Finals was Wanderers. Their hat-trick came in 1876, 1877 and 1878 after two earlier appearances in 1872 and 1873. They won all five.

The first F.A. Cup was stolen in 1895 and never recovered. The present trophy was made by a Bradford silversmith in 1911 and was won for the first time by Bradford City.

Paul Allen at 17 years 256 days was the youngest F.A. Cup Finalist when he played for West Ham against Arsenal in 1979-80. The Hammers had also produced the youngest scorer . . . John Sissons against Preston in 1964 when he was 18 years 215 days old.

Walter Hampson at 41 years eight months old was the oldest Finalist when he appeared for Newcastle United against Aston Villa in 1924.

APPEARANCES IN WEMBLEY FINALS 1923-1982

Arsenal	**11 (5)**
Manchester City	**7 (3)**
Manchester United	**7 (3)**
Newcastle United	**6 (5)**
Bolton Wanderers	**5 (4)**
Liverpool	**5 (2)**
Leeds United	**4 (1)**
Leicester City	**4 (0)**
Preston North End	**4 (1)**
Tottenham Hotspur	**5 (5)**
West Bromwich Albion	**4 (3)**
West Ham United	**4 (3)**
Blackpool	**3 (1)**
Everton	**3 (2)**
Huddersfield Town	**3 (0)**
Portsmouth	**3 (1)**
Wolverhampton Wanderers	**3 (2)**
Aston Villa	**2 (1)**

Magic

Birmingham City	**2 (0)**
Blackburn Rovers	**2 (1)**
Burnley	**2 (0)**
Cardiff City	**2 (1)**
Charlton Athletic	**2 (1)**
Chelsea	**2 (1)**
Sheffield United	**2 (1)**
Sheffield Wednesday	**2 (1)**
Sunderland	**2 (2)**
Derby County	**1 (1)**
Fulham	**1 (0)**
Ipswich	**1 (1)**
Luton Town	**1 (0)**
Nottingham Forest	**1 (1)**
Southampton	**1 (1)**
Q.P.R.	**1 (0)**

(wins in brackets)

Chief Joseph

The Napoleon of the Redmen

The Indian Chief who held the United States Army at bay

Thunder-Rolling-Over-the-Mountain, or Chief Joseph as he was called by the white man, was undoubtedly the greatest of all fighting chiefs. This chieftain of the Nez Perce tribe was the Napoleon of the Redmen. His brilliant leadership against two thousand white soldiers dumbfounded the United States Army.

The Nez Perce War was the most extraordinary Red Indian campaign in history. For forty years the Nez Perces had lived peaceably in the Wallows Valley, Oregon. They were an extremely intelligent and advanced tribe.

Because the great chieftain loved his people he did everything possible to avert bloodshed and war. He put up with endless insults from the whites. But when the Government threatened to put the Nez Perces on a reservation, some of his warriors rebelled,

The heart of Thunder-Rolling-Over-the-Mountain was heavy for he knew there was no turning back. It was war. He had never before fired a gun or shot an arrow in anger, and yet with only three hundred armed warriors he fought the soldiers.

The soldiers found themselves up against a clever and civilised enemy commander. Chief Joseph taught his warriors to ride in cavalry formation. He employed advance and rear guards. When making a stand, he dug trenches or formed breastworks.
Thunder-Rolling-Over-the-Mountain decided to cross into Canada. His tribe would be safe there, but the long march meant fighting all the way. The courage of his warriors was unsurpassed.
Determined to capture the Nez Perces, General Howard telegraphed army posts all over the northwest, and troops began closing in on the Redskins. To delay Howard's troops, the chieftain planned a night attack to stampede the pack mules.
While his scouts were silencing the sentries, Thunder-Rolling-Over-the-Mountain and the rest of his warriors slow-trotted towards the sleeping camp. They sounded just like a cavalry patrol. Suddenly they charged and stampeded the mules.

Without pack mules General Howard was unable to pursue the Nez Perces who struggled northwards. But there was no respite, for General Gibbon attacked them two mornings later.

To give his weary people time to move in safety, Thunder-Rolling-Over-the-Mountain set light to the grassy strip in front of the soldiers, placing a blazing ring of fire between them.

By the time Gibbon's troops had fought the fire, the Nez Perces were miles away. The Redskins, however, were utterly exhausted. Canada was only 30 miles away when disaster — in the form of General Miles and his cavalry — overtook them.

The exhausted Redskins put up a desperate fight, but when General Howard joined General Miles, the intrepid chief knew he was beaten at last. Sadly, with hope dead in his heart, Thunder-Rolling-Over-the-Mountain surrendered.

THE ROBBER 'GHOST'

The word was out: Will Nevison was taken. The famous Yorkshire highwayman was lodged in Leicester gaol, securely fettered and strongly guarded. Escape was impossible, and his friends came to pay their last respects. One of his friends was a physician, who revealed that Nevison was infected with the plague and that, unless he was given fresh air, he would die and infect the whole gaol.

Prisons in the 17th century were breeding grounds for plague; previous epidemics had taken a heavy toll of the prison officers. Consequently, Nevison was quickly removed to a cell of his own. The doctor came every day, but his condition worsened. Soon Nevison's face and hands were covered in blue spots — the harbingers of impending death. An anaesthetic was administered and, shortly afterwards, the doctor informed the officials that his patient had died.

A jury, summoned to determine the cause of death, took one look at the blue spots, and brought in their verdict: death by the plague. The doctor arranged for the body to be taken away and buried. It seemed that Will Nevison had cheated the hangman.

Then, the night after Nevison's supposed burial, a traveller was held up and robbed on one of the highwayman's old stamping grounds. It was not so much the highwayman's pistols which terrified the traveller, but the highwayman himself: the man swore it was Will Nevison back from the dead. The same thing happened a few nights later. It appeared that travellers were being robbed by Nevison's ghost.

What had actually happened was one of the most ingenious escapes in history. Nevison's friend, posing as a doctor, had painted on the blue spots; the "anaesthetic" had been a strong sleeping draught which had rendered the "patient" unconscious for some hours. In the panic caused by the very mention of the word, "plague", the prison officials had only taken a cursory look at the prisoner's body.

For many long months afterwards, Will Nevison made great play on his victims' fear of the supernatural, for the terror his ghostly appearance produced made highway robbery much simpler.

William Nevison was born in Pontefract, Yorkshire, in 1639. When about 14 years of age, he stole a silver spoon from his father. Instead of himself punishing the boy, Mr. Nevison transferred the task to Will's schoolmaster, who thrashed him severely. As a result, Will decided to run away from home. Helping himself to £10 from his father's cash box, and a saddle and bridle from his father's stable, he then rode off to London on his schoolmaster's horse.

In London, young Nevison worked for a brewer for three years, after which he stole £200 and left the country. In Flanders, he enlisted in one of the English regiments in the Spanish service under the command of the Duke of York (later James II). After a time he deserted and returned to England, where he decided to become a highwayman.

One day, shortly after Will "took to the road", he met two farmers, who advised him it was dangerous to travel, as they had just been robbed of £40 by three highwaymen only half a mile off. Telling the farmers to follow him, Nevison started off in pursuit of the robbers.

Impetuous

Shortly afterwards, the money was returned to the delighted farmers. The impetuous Nevison had held up the three highwaymen and, shooting one of them in the arm, had obtained all of their day's "takings". Nevison was well satisfied with his own day's work, for the farmers had not been the only people the three highwaymen had robbed that day and Will was the richer by over £100.

This was one of the few documented occasions when one highwayman held up other highwaymen and it was, of course, very much against the code. Nevison was, however, new to the profession, and still had to learn the finer points of behaviour that befitted a "gentleman of the road".

After being a few years "on the road", Nevison made a modest fortune, and decided to return home. His family received him with open arms. He lived quietly in the country for a while, until his need for more money and more adventures urged him once more to take up the life of the horse and pistol.

Daring

Nevison became famous all over the North of England for his daring robberies and, especially, for his generosity to the poor. He was not so popular, however, with the drovers and graziers, who had to pay him protection money.

By 1674, Nevison appears to have gathered a small army of highwaymen around him, for a pamphlet, published that year, entitled "Bloody News from Yorkshire", described a pitched battle between 15 butchers riding to Northallerton Fair, and Will Nevison and 20 of his men.

Shortly after his famed escape from Leicester gaol, Nevison was nearly caught again. Staying at an inn which had always afforded him refuge in the past, he was given drugged beer. The innkeeper, Darcy Fletcher, paid for his treachery. The drugged beer failed to render Nevison unconscious, and he fought his way out of the trap, killing Fletcher with a pistol shot.

It was another innkeeper, a woman, who was to bring about his final capture. At midnight on 6th March, 1684, in his room at the Plough Inn, Sandal, near Wakefield, Nevison was rudely awakened by three men: the constable, his assistant and an army officer who lived nearby. He was securely bound and taken to York Castle.

Despite his insistence that Charles II had given him a royal pardon, Nevison was found guilty and was hanged at York on 18th March, 1684.

Legion

Colonel Klicki's Polish Lancers could see the carnage that was going on outside the little Spanish town of Albuera. One division of French infantry had been caught in the flank by some British regiments under Col. Colborne while the French were still fighting Spanish infantry to their front.

Volley after volley poured into the packed French ranks from only sixty paces. Then Colborne's men cheered loudly and rushed forward to finish their foes with the

d'Honneur

bayonet. What happened next was one of the worst disasters that the British Army suffered in its long struggle against Napoleon's legions in Spain.

Wiped out

On a hill to the west, Latour-Maubourg, one of Napoleon's best cavalry generals now chose his moment to attack. As the British infantry charged, he sent Col. Klicki's Polish Lancers and a regiment of French Hussars forward. Hidden by clouds of gunpowder smoke that billowed from the infantry battle and by squalls of rain that suddenly lashed the battlefield, Latour-Maubourg's eight hundred horsemen crashed into the enemy's unprotected flank. Three British battalions were almost wiped out in three minutes, before they had time to form defensive squares.

Charge!

The Polish horsemen of the 1st Regiment of Vistula Lancers swept onwards right through the British infantry. Even Sir William Beresford, who commanded the Allied British and Spanish army, only saved himself by pushing aside a Polish lance with his bare hands. Still the lancers and hussars charged on until they reached the Allied artillery and some British reinforcements who were hurrying up from the rear.

The Polish Lancers were particularly effective and ruthless among the disorganized foot-soldiers. Incredible heroism was shown by both sides. The wounded colonel of the British 57th Infantry Regiment, for example, lay amid his men shouting, "Die hard, 57th! Die hard!" This unit later became the Middlesex Regiment who are still known as the Diehards. The Poles captured five of the six flags belonging to these three battalions, plus almost five hundred prisoners, four guns and a huge howitzer. But by the end of that savage day, 16th May, 1811, the Allied British and Spanish armies still won the cruel battle of Albuera. Nevertheless, the Poles deserved the Legion d'Honneur that was given to the 1st Regiment of Vistula Lancers three months later.

Roll of honour

This famous medal was created by Napoleon Bonaparte in 1802, and although most of those who earned the right to wear its ten-pointed white cross have been Frenchmen, many other nations are also represented in its roll of honour. Some fifty years after Albuera, Egyptian troops marched with a French expeditionary force to Mexico and a number of their officers earned the Legion d'Honneur. During the First World War many of France's allies also won this, the highest of French decorations, including the leading fighter ace of the Belgian Air Force, Willy Coppens.

Over the years many different portrait heads have been placed at the centre of the beautiful Legion d'Honneur cross, including Napoleon himself and the warrior-king, Henry IV of France. Today this medal bears the allegorical figurehead of France, but all these versions of the Legion d'Honneur have retained the blood-red ribbon of what remains one of the world's most famous decorations.

The Ghost of Boulder City

AT LAST, THE FISSURE OPENED OUT INTO A SECONDARY SHAFT... AND ATTRACTED BY A GLEAM OF LIGHT, CALVIN RAN ON. UNTIL SUDDENLY
FOUND THEM, BY GLORY— ALL OF THEM! DAZED AND SEMI-CONSCIOUS, BUT STILL BREATHING!
AND, LATER...
YOU CAN BE PROUD OF YOURSELF, BOY! THANKS TO THAT ROUTE YOU FOUND, ALL TWELVE HAVE BEEN SAVED!
TWELVE? BUT WHEN I WAS CHECKING TO SEE IF THEY WERE ALL THERE I COUNTED THIRTEEN!
WELL, I KNOW FOR A FACT THERE WERE ONLY TWELVE MEN WORKIN' THAT SHIFT... AND ALL OF THEM ARE SAFE IN THE WAGON!
IT DOESN'T MAKE SENSE! THERE WERE THIRTEEN MINERS DOWN THERE—I'M POSITIVE!
SHIVERING, CALVIN THOUGHT AGAIN, OF THAT GRIM AND TERRIBLE SCENE...
COME TO THINK OF IT, THERE WAS ONE MAN I HADN'T SEEN BEFORE! AN OLD MAN WITH A RAGGED WHITE BEARD! HE'S THE THIRTEENTH MAN!
DEEPLY PUZZLED, CALVIN MADE HIS WAY BACK TO TOWN. THEN SUDDENLY...
AL STORE
EARL CARTER PROPRIETOR
THERE HE IS, BY THUNDER! NOW I'M GONNA SOLVE THIS MYSTERY ONCE AND FOR ALL!

BUT...
A DEAD-END! AND THE OLD MAN'S GONE — VANISHED INTO THIN AIR!
THAT NIGHT, CALVIN PUZZLED OVER THE MYSTERY...
IF ONLY I COULD EXPLAIN THAT DISAPPEARING TRICK! BUT I CAN'T! THE WHOLE THING IS SO UNREAL IT BORDERS ON THE UNCANNY!
RESTLESS, HE DRESSED AND OPENED THE WINDOW. AND...
UP THERE ON THE MOUNTAIN! IT'S HIM — THE THIRTEENTH MAN! ARMS REACHING TOWARDS THE STARS!
THE BOY KNEW THEN THAT SOMETHING TERRIBLE WAS ABOUT TO HAPPEN! IT WAS AN INTUITION THAT SENT HIM RUNNING INTO THE NIGHT, YELLING...
WAKE UP! EVERYONE WAKE UP! GET DRESSED AND RUN! RUN FOR YOUR LIVES!
WHAT IN TARNATION..? THAT'S YOUNG McCORD, AIN'T IT? SOMEBODY GET THE SHERIFF!
UNION BANK
HARDWARE
STAR
HOTE
EASY, BOY, JUST SIMMER DOWN! YOU GONE LOCO OR SOMETHIN'?
Y-YOU MUST GET EVERYBODY OUT OF TOWN, SHERIFF, FAST! I CAN'T EXPLAIN WHY, BUT THERE'S GOING TO BE A DISASTER! I KNOW THERE IS!
MURPHY'S
SUDDENLY...
YAAA-HAIEEE!
KA-ZZAMP!

BRRRMMMBLE!
A THUNDERBOLT HAS STRUCK THE MOUNTAIN! CALVIN McCORD WAS RIGHT!
FRR-RUUMP!
THAT LANDSLIDE WILL BURY THE ENTIRE TOWN! RUN FOR IT WHILE YOU CAN!
MEN! WOMEN! CHILDREN! ANIMALS! ALL FLED TOGETHER FROM THE FURY OF THE MOUNTAIN!
KRAASH!
KER-RUNCH!
AND WHEN DAWN BROKE... BOULDER CITY WAS NO MORE!
SHUCKS, I'VE NEVER SEEN SUCH A MESS! OUR TOWN HAS BEEN WIPED OFF THE FACE OF THE EARTH!
YEAH, BUT THANKS TO CALVIN'S PREMONITION, AT LEAST OUR LIVES WERE SAVED, SHERIFF! AND I, FOR ONE, AM MIGHTY GRATEFUL!
HOTEL
CALVIN SUDDENLY FROZE AS HE SAW A CRACKED AND FADED PHOTOGRAPH LYING AT HIS FEET...
HOWLIN' COYOTES, THIS MUST HAVE BEEN THROWN CLEAR WHEN THE HOTEL COLLAPSED! IT'S A FRAMED PHOTO OF THAT MYSTERIOUS OLD MAN!

MYSTERIOUS? WHY I KNEW HIM... THE POOR GUY DIED OVER TEN YEARS AGO! CALLED HIMSELF TUMBLEWEED SMITH!
"WHEN GOLD WAS DISCOVERED, THE MINERS DROVE HIM OFF HIS FARM AND GRABBED HIS LAND. TUMBLEWEED SWORE THEN THAT ONE DAY HE'D GET HIS REVENGE...
FROM THIS DAY FORTH, I CURSE THE NAME OF BOULDER CITY AND ALL WHO LIVE IN IT! VENGEANCE SHALL BE MINE!
HA, HA, HA! GO AN' MAKE YOUR THREATS SOMEWHERE ELSE, OLD-TIMER! YOU'RE ALL WASHED UP!
"...THE END CAME ONE DAY HIGH ON THE MOUNTAIN. IN A FRENZY OF RAGE, TUMBLEWEED CHASED OFF TWO MINERS... BUT THEN SLIPPED AND FELL TO HIS DOOM..."
YEEEAAAARGH!
AND THERE THE STORY ENDS, CALVIN! THE OLD GUY NEVER DID LIVE LONG ENOUGH TO GET HIS REVENGE!
PERHAPS NOT... BUT HE FINALLY CLAIMED HIS VENGEANCE AFTER HE DIED! YESTERDAY MORNING I SAW THE GHOST OF TUMBLEWEED SMITH—FREED AT LAST BY THE EXPLOSION IN THE MOUNTAIN!
THERE CAN BE NO OTHER ANSWER TO THE MYSTERY OF THE THIRTEENTH MAN, OR THE THUNDERBOLT THAT CAME SO SWIFTLY FROM A CLEAR NIGHT SKY!
BOULDER CITY IS GONE FOREVER... AND TUMBLEWEED SMITH HAS FOUND PEACE AT LAST!
THE END

Not all of Britain's many phantoms are spectres with clanking chains, or wraiths that walk through solid walls. There are other horrors that lurk in wait for the unwary — but perhaps the most grisly is the skull that hovers in the air, or, when touched, gives vent to a blood-curdling shriek!

You don't believe there are such things?

You're wrong. There are quite a few of them!

One of the most famous of these "screaming skulls" is that of a negro slave, who was brought to England from the West Indies about 200 years ago by his master, a former exile who returned to Bettiscombe, a few miles from Lyme Regis, Dorset.

The climate of England did not suit the slave. He sickened and died, after extracting a promise from his master that his body would be sent back to his homeland.

For some reason, the promise was never fulfilled. He was interred in a Bettiscombe graveyard — all of him, that is, except for his head, which was cut off and kept in the house, though nobody nowadays knows why.

Attempts have sometimes been made, over the years, to unite the skull with the dead slave's skeleton, and to carry out his wishes. Yet it seems that his desire to have a resting-place in the West Indies was not entirely sincere.

Each time the skull has been taken from its niche in the farmhouse, blood-curdling yells have echoed through the rooms. Cattle have died, crops have failed, and life in the village has become intolerable.

Torments of this kind have not ended until the horrible article has been restored to its niche — so to make this state of affairs more permanent, it was protected from further moves by bricking up the niche where it lay.

Later residents of the farm have respected the queer custom, taking little or no notice of the existence of the skull so close to them. On the other hand, no one has braved the fearful risks said to be involved in disturbing the skull, either by burying it in Bettiscombe graveyard, or by sending it back to the West Indies.

REVENGE

Some skulls are far more malevolent, and are said to scream out for revenge.

For instance, a field near Ambleside, in the Lake District, is thick with boulders, and among them are two stones like decayed human heads which are said to scream if they are moved — or even if they are about to be moved.

The story goes that a farmhouse stood on the field 200 years ago. A wealthy neighbour wanted the farm, but the owner and his wife refused to sell.

The rich man invited them to a banquet, and instructed a servant to slip a silver trinket into the farmer's pocket, secretly. Later, the item was reported missing — and everyone present was searched.

The trinket was of course found in the farmer's garment, and he and his wife were sentenced to death — theft being a capital offence in those days.

The wife put a curse on the rich man before she was hanged, declaring that he would never know rest until the end of his life. From that day on, the ghostly heads of the two unfortunates appeared from time to time at the top of the stairs in the rich man's house, and in the rooms of any premises he occupied. Frequently, blood-curdling screams were heard.

The strain proved too much for him, and he sickened and died. His descendants, anxious to overcome the curse, are said to have dug up the corpses of the farmer and his wife, severed the heads from their bodies, and thrown the skulls among the boulders in the field.

Their ability to scream, however, is reputed to be unimpaired, and horrifying noises are said to be heard at dead of night by anybody passing the field.

CHURCHYARD HOWLS

Another country property which is the setting for a screaming skull is Higher Chilton Manor Farm, Somerset. Workmen carrying out alterations there in 1826 had a morbid custom of drinking beer from a human skull, kept in a casket placed over the front door, believing that this action would improve their strength.

The skull they used had a sinister history. According to the villagers, it was the bony head of a Warwickshire man who had fled to Somerset to escape punishment for his activities in the Civil War.

His name was Theophilus Brome, and he settled into the manor farm, where he eventually made a death-bed wish that his skull should be kept in the house. Today, a relic of this kind is kept in a special cabinet above the entrance to the farmstead.

However, the story goes, the instructions were not at first carried out, and after he was buried horrifying yells and howls began to be heard in the vicinity of the churchyard. Nor did they cease until ex-soldier Brome's wishes were strictly observed.

Although he had been buried unmutilated, his grave was opened and his head cut off, so that it could be placed in a special cabinet over the entrance to the farm.

There was a remarkable sequel to this story — for the grave was re-opened to test the truth of the tale in the middle of the 18th Century. Sure enough, the skeleton was found to be headless. So the skull over the farmhouse doorway is most probably that of Theophilus Brome.

HEADLESS MONK

The poet Lord Byron refers in one of his poems to a spectre resembling a monk which he conjured up by turning a human skull into a drinking vessel, at a dinner party in Newstead Abbey, Nottinghamshire. The improvised cup had no sooner been filled with wine than a headless figure dressed in monkish robes appeared, and warned the poet of disasters to come, as a result of disturbing the old graves of the Abbey.

The skull had, in fact, been dug up during an escapade by Byron and some friends, and the curses which the monk uttered mostly came true. Only a month later, Byron entered into a period of profound melancholia, which he blamed on the phantom.

Unfortunately, the curse was not lifted when he left the Abbey, other occupants suffering from it. Although the skull was not a screaming one, it was considered responsible for several tragedies, including a drowning, the untimely death of a Cambridge student, and the unexpected succumbing of an explorer and military expert who perished in East Africa.

In an attempt to lift the curse, the skull was reburied in the monastery ruins. Since then, things have been somewhat calmer around Newstead Abbey.

IMPALED

Only eight miles from Manchester stands Wardley Hall, once the home of a boisterous young man called Roger Downe. A strange and contradictory tale is told about a skull said to belong to him.

The horrified rich man was haunted by the shrieking, ghostly heads of the unfortunates he had sent to their death.

When ex-soldier Brome's coffin was dug up, it was discovered that his skeleton was headless.

The story goes that he was killed in a brawl on Old London Bridge, when he and some companions attacked the watchman. Shouts brought support for the beleaguered guardian from passers-by, and one of these decapitated Roger with a mighty blow. The gory head was put in a box and sent to Wardley Hall, where Roger's sister placed it in a niche overlooking the staircase.

Attempts to give it a Christian burial have always failed, its removal from the house having been followed by screams and screeches so distressing that it has quickly been returned to its accustomed niche.

Another account states that Roger was not a thief but a hero, accidentally slain while trying to protect the London Bridge watchman from attack, and that his head was sent back to Wardley Hall by admirers of his bravery.

TUDOR TIMES

A different tale, however, is that the relic is all that remains of a monk, Ambrose Barlow, who perished in the religious upheavals of Tudor times. After being found guilty of heresy, he was executed at Lancaster in 1641 and his head was impaled outside a Manchester church.

Friends rescued the head, however, and put it into the care of the Downe family, at Wardley Hall, who preserved it secretly and spread the London Bridge story as a precaution, in case the skull was found by enemies. In those days of religious persecution it would have been most unwise for a monk's head to have been found in the home of the Downe family, as it would have revealed their sympathy for a banned form of worship.

To this day, a clause in the documents relating to the legal standing of Wardley Hall forbids the removal of "a skull, alleged to be that of a martyr"

LOUD SCREAMS

Yorkshire has a famous screaming skull in a niche at Burton Agnes Hall, a beautiful Jacobean house visible from the main road between Bridlington and Driffield.

The head is said to be that of Anne Griffith, daughter of the first owner of the Hall. "Aud Nance", as the villagers call her ghost today, was attacked by a tramp near Burton Agnes, and, although mortally injured, she lingered a few days before dying.

On her deathbed, she repeatedly asked that her head be kept in the Hall for as long as the building stood. To pacify Anne, her sisters told her they would do this, but later disregarded her deathbed wish, and the murdered girl was buried in the normal way.

A week later the occupants of the Hall were disturbed by continual thuds and bangs, and loud screams, throughout the night, and the tumult was repeated until one of Anne's sisters remembered the dead girl's request.

As soon as her skull was dug up, and brought into the mansion, the disturbances ceased. Later residents have had the relic removed at various times, either deliberately or unintentionally, but each time the old commotions have started again, continuing until the skull has been replaced in its niche.

Yet one aspect of life at Burton Agnes Hall was beyond the control of "Aud Nance". She could not prevent the present-day owners of the Hall from turning the mansion into a 20th Century showplace.

Despite its chilling associations, it attracts crowds of tourists — though no one has heard any wild and blood-curdling shrieks for many a long day!

FOR VALOUR

Men can often fight as bravely in bad causes as they can in good ones. When Mussolini threw the ill-equipped and unprepared Italian Army against Greece in 1940, he expected the invasion to be a walk-over. The Fascist Dictator told his soldiers so, and many of them believed him. Some did not, however, and others were soon to learn just what an impossible task their blustering leader had set them.

Not only did the Italians face a tough foe but the autumn weather in the bleak mountains of the Greek-Albanian border also turned against them.

Medaglia d'Oro

Everywhere men slogged forward through mud and rain, along tracks that were only suitable for goats. Even down near the Mediterranean coast conditions were not much better.

Here, on October 28th 1940, the Italians were held up by the Kalamas river. Normally this was a small stream but now, swollen by the storms, it was seventy metres wide, three metres deep, and carried the debris of blown-up bridges and drowned animals. This was the obstacle that faced Lieutenant Riccardi Avati of the Aosta Lancers who commanded a patrol some way ahead of the rest of the army.

Man after man fell. No less than seven Victoria Crosses were awarded that day.

Among his men were some good swimmers who volunteered to go forward. But Avati knew that any man who went first would be a sitting duck if the Greeks saw him from the other side of the river. Clearly it was a job that he had to do himself. So Lt. Avati hid his horse in a nearby wood and took off his uniform. Gripping his pistol between his teeth, the young Italian officer struggled through the raging torrent. More than once he was almost swept down to the sea but eventually he got to the other side and after checking that all was clear, told the rest of his platoon to cross. Soon another detachment arrived, and together with Avati's men made a tiny raft on which they pulled three machine-guns across the Kalamas river. Not until November 5th was a bridge of boats built by Italian Army engineers, but by then Lt. Avati's fragile bridgehead was securely held.

That was as far as the Italian Army got in 1940. Lt. Avati went forward to reconnoitre the little town of Igoumenitsa and was killed in a skirmish with the enemy. Later his family heard that he had been awarded the Medaglia d'Oro, Italy's highest bravery award, for his solo crossing of the Kalamas. Perhaps Lt. Avati was lucky. He did not have to see the humiliating rout that the Italians were soon to suffer at the hands of their Greek enemies.

The Gold Medal for Valour has a long history that reflects Italy's hard struggle for unity and independence. The ancient Kingdom of Savoy, which was to become the nucleus of a new Italy, started giving gold medals for courage in 1793 but they were abandoned when Napoleon occupied the country. In 1815 these first gold medals were replaced by the Military Order of Savoy. Then, in 1833, King Charles Albert reintroduced the gold Medaglia d'Oro al Valore Militare. With this medal came a welcome increase in pay for any who earned it.

The Medaglia d'Oro was later inherited by the Kingdom of Italy following the unification of the country. So was the Naval Medaglia d'Oro, established in 1836. In 1927 a similar medal was created for the Air Force, and there was even a fourth version for civilians. All these medals had slightly different ribbons. When Italy became a republic after the Second World War, the only change in these various Gold Medals for Valour was the disappearance of the royal crown and its replacement by a republican emblem.

TIGER OF THE DEEP
CAUGHT IN THE TAIL-END WINDS OF A HURRICANE, LOUIS BERNARD AND HIS NEPHEW, TOD MASSEY, ABOARD THEIR LAUNCH CATARACT, WERE BATTERED BY THE GIANT SEAS THAT POUNDED CARIBOU BAY . . . AND THEN, CLOSE TO LAND, THEIR DINGHY WAS SWEPT OVERBOARD . . .
LOOK . . . THERE'S OUR DINGHY!
PORT YOUR HELM, TOD . . . GO NO NEARER! THOSE WHIRLPOOLS WOULD DEVOUR AN OCEAN LINER IF IT GOT WITHIN THEIR CLUTCHES!
CATARACT
THE DOOMED DINGHY SPUN FASTER . . . NEARING THE CENTRE OF THE SPINNING WATER . . .
UNTIL IT WAS SUCKED UNDER . . . DOWN . . . DOWN TO THE BONE-CRUSHING PRESSURES BELOW . . .
THE CATARACT, MINUS ITS DINGHY, LIMPED TOWARDS HOME . . .
I THINK THE WEATHER'S BEGINNING TO EASE, UNCLE LOUIS. THE WIND'S DROPPING.
YOU ARE RIGHT. STEER TWO POINTS FURTHER TO THE EAST . . . SOON WE WILL BE IN THE CALM WATERS OF THE HARBOUR . . .
TWO DAYS LATER THE CATARACT WAS REPAIRED AND LOUIS BERNARD WAS RENEWING THE BROKEN GEAR . . .
WHAT'S GOING ON HERE?
THEY SOUND ANGRY.
PAINT
WHY THE MEETING, MY FRIEND? IS ANYTHING WRONG?
JON CALETTE, THE OLD MAN WHO OWNS THE KESTREL, IS LOST AT SEA, BERNARD . . . AND IT'S ALL ON ACCOUNT OF THAT DARN KILLER FISH, SCARBACK . . .

WELL, SCARBACK AIN'T GOING TO GET AWAY WITH IT, SEE! WE'RE GONNA HUNT IT DOWN . . . WITH GRENADES AND MORTAR SHELLS. WE AIN'T FISHING THIS TIME . . . WE'RE PLAYING FOR KEEPS!
SCARBACK WON'T STAND A CHANCE . . . THEY'LL BLOW HIM TO PIECES . . .
FIRST RANSOME MUST FIND HIM! AND THAT WON'T BE EASY. BUT I DO NOT LIKE THEIR METHODS . . . EVEN OLD JON CALETTE WOULD NOT WISH TO BE AVENGED IN THIS FASHION . . .
AN HOUR LATER . . .
ALL GONE FOR'D, UNCLE LOUIS . . .
THEN LET US GO . . . MAYBE IT IS NOT YET TOO LATE FOR US TO CATCH SCARBACK . . . WITH ROD AND LINE . . .
THE CATARACT SURGED FORWARD ACROSS THE PLACID WATERS OF THE PACIFIC, UNTIL . . .
WRECKAGE AHEAD!
STAND BY TO PICK IT UP, TOD . . .
LOOK . . . PART OF THE BOWS . . . OF JON CALETTE'S SHIP . . . THE KESTREL!
IT'S PROBABLY DRIFTED SOME WAY . . . THE CURRENT HERE SETS FROM THE WEST. WE'LL TAKE THAT COURSE . . . IT MAY BRING US TO SCARBACK!
KESTREL
LESS THAN TWO HOURS LATER . . .
LOOK! SCARBACK!
BREAK OUT THE HEAVY TACKLE . . . GET THE BAIT OVER THE SIDE. THIS MAY BE OUR LAST CHANCE TO CATCH HIM . . . BEFORE THE GRENADE BOYS ARRIVE!

THERE HE GOES . . . HE'S TAKING THE BAIT!
IF HE TAKES THE HOOK, TOO . . . WE'VE GOT A FIGHT ON OUR HANDS . . . THE BIGGEST FIGHT OF OUR LIVES!
SUDDENLY, LOUIS WAS JERKED SAVAGELY FORWARD INTO HIS HARNESS STRAPS . . . THE LINE SCREAMED THROUGH THE REEL . . . SCARBACK WAS HOOKED!
YOU'VE GOT HIM!
NOW I HAVE TO HOLD HIM. PLAY HIM UNTIL HE TIRES . . . OR I TIRE AND LOSE HIM!
THE GIANT TIGER-SHARK TRIED EVERYTHING TO ESCAPE . . . TOWING CATARACT MILES OFF COURSE . . .
UNCLE LOUIS . . . THERE'S A MAN. ON THAT ROCK! IT — IT'S OLD JON CALETTE!
CATARACT
WHAT ABOUT SCARBACK?
LET HIM GO FOR NOW. I'LL LET OUT ALL THE LINE. FIRST WE MUST HELP OLD JON!
SLOWLY, LOUIS BERNARD SLID THE LAUNCH STERN-FIRST BETWEEN THE SUCKING WHIRLPOOLS . . .
JUMP, JON . . . JUMP FOR THE STERN AS SOON AS WE'RE NEAR ENOUGH!
HAVE A CARE, MR. BERNARD . . . ONE INCH OFF COURSE AND YOU'LL BE IN THE WHIRLPOOLS AND THAT IS DEATH!

AND THEN . . .
HE'S GONE IN. KEEP HER STEADY, TOD!
AAARRGGHHH!
LOUIS BERNARD'S STEELY FINGERS GRASPED THE OLD MAN'S SHOULDER . . .
OKAY, TOD . . . I'VE GOT HIM. GO SLOW AHEAD. LET'S GET OUT OF HERE BEFORE THE CURRENTS DRIFT US INTO THE WHIRLPOOL . . .
THEY STRUGGLED ABOARD . . .
THE WHEEL, TOD!
LEAVE ME . . . I – I CAN MANAGE . . .
TOO LATE . . . THE TREACHEROUS GRIP OF THE WHIRLING WATER HAD THEM IN ITS POWER . . .
FULL AHEAD, TOD . . . GET EVERY OUNCE OUT OF THOSE ENGINES!
IT – IT IS TOO LATE, LOUIS . . . ONCE THE WHIRLPOOL GRIPS ITS VICTIM . . . IT NEVER LETS GO . . . NEVER!
SEE! WE GET NEARER THE CENTRE . . .
THERE'S ONE HOPE! SCARBACK! IF HE'S STILL ON THE END OF THE LINE . . .
DESPERATELY LOUIS BERNARD REELED IN THE LINE, UNTIL . . .
CATARACT
HE'S STILL THERE! OUR ONLY CHANCE NOW . . . IS THE STRENGTH OF SCARBACK!
BY THUNDER, SCARBACK'S DOING IT. HE'S PULLING US CLEAR. HANG ON, LOUIS . . . HANG ON!
I MUST . . . JUST – JUST A LITTLE LONGER . . .

AND THEN . . .
WE'RE SAFE! THE BIG FISH HAS SAVED US!
HE'S BEGINNING TO TIRE, TOO . . . EVEN FOR HIM TO STRAIN OF THE FIGHT WITH A WHIRLPOOL IS ENOUGH!
YARD BY YARD, LOUIS BEGAN TO REEL IN THE LINE . . .
HE CAN'T GET AWAY NOW . . . WE HAVE HIM!
UNCLE LOUIS, LOOK! RANSOME AND HIS MEN!
THE GRENADE BOYS!
HEY, RANSOME . . . THAT'S THE CATARACT. LOOKS LIKE BERNARD'S HOOKED SCARBACK.
GOOD! STAND BY WITH THE GRENADES AND MORTARS. BERNARD MAY HAVE HOOKED HIM . . . BUT WE'LL FINISH HIM OFF!
ON THE CATARACT . . .
THEY'VE COME TO AVENGE YOU, JON . . . WITH EXPOSIVES! SCARBACK IS FINISHED!
BUT IT WAS NOT SCARBACK WHO SANK MY SHIP. I RADIOED THAT I'D SIGHTED HIM . . . AND THEN I HIT A REEF. THE SHIP'S BOTTOM WAS TORN OUT . . . I HAD NO TIME FOR A FURTHER MESSAGE . . .
I CAN'T STAND BY AND SEE SCARBACK BLOWN TO PIECES . . . LET'S GIVE HIM A CHANCE, EH, JON?
I'M WITH YOU, LOUIS . . . HE SAVED OUR LIVES . . . WE SAVE HIS!
AFTER LOUIS HAD CUT THE LINE, ALLOWING SCARBACK TO ESCAPE, HE PUT ON A FRESH HOOK AND CAST FOR SOME ROCKS.
JUST TO MAKE SURE . . . THIS SHOULD FOOL THEM.

THEN, RANSOME AND HIS MEN WERE THERE . . .
JUST KEEP A – HOLDING HIM, BERNARD . . . ME AND MY BOYS WILL DO THE REST.
OKAY . . . I WON'T LET GO!
THE THREE LAUNCHES BACKED AROUND . . .
OKAY, ALL OF YOU . . . OPEN FIRE! DROP 'EM AROUND THAT REEF. SCARBACK'S SKULKING DOWN THERE SOMEWHERE!
NOTHING COULD HAVE LIVED IN THAT DELUGE OF DEATH!
THAT'S ENOUGH! HOLD IT! YOU CAN SAY GOODBYE TO SCARBACK, BOYS . . . HE'S HAD IT!
WE FOUND JON CALETTE, TOO . . . HE IS SAFE!
WELL, AIN'T THAT JUST GREAT! NICE DAY'S WORK, LOUIS . . . SEE YOU BACK IN HARBOUR!
WELL, TIME WE TURNED FOR HOME, TOO, JON. BUT WE'LL BE BACK . . . AND NEXT TIME, MAYBE . . . WE CATCH SCARBACK . . .
HE IS A WORTHY OPPONENT, LOUIS . . .
BUT SCARBACK IS A FISH . . . AND SHOULD BE CAUGHT BY FISHERMAN . . . NOT EXPLOSIVES!
YOU ARE RIGHT, MY FRIEND!

Last of

To him, it was a lucrative game. To his victims, it was an expensive entertainment. To history, it was — romance!

Far and wide the Wild Bunch ranged, often in a band of as many as 100 riders.

the Fast Guns

They say he could drill six shots through the ace on a playing card at 20 paces with a Colt revolver. An artist with a lariat, an expert ranch hand, one of the best horsemen who ever mounted a western saddle, Robert LeRoy Parker was a man who succeeded at everything he tried.

Small wonder that, when he turned to a life of crime under the alias "Butch Cassidy", Robert LeRoy Parker became one of the most successful outlaws in the history of the American frontier.

Trail

Butch had already completed his apprenticeship as a horse thief and cattle rustler while still in his teens. And he went on from there to blaze a trail as a bandit across the wild west.

As outlaws go, Butch Cassidy was an exception to many rules. Throughout a 17-year crime spree which included hundreds of robberies and plenty of gunplay, Butch was never known to have killed a man. An easy-going, happy-go-lucky sort, he had a quick grin and a ready wit which won him friends everywhere. What's more, he was a bandit with a well-developed sense of humour.

While serving a two-year prison term for stealing horses in Wyoming, Cassidy was summoned to the office of the Governor of the state to discuss a pardon. The Governor told him, "Butch, we'll let you free if you'll give me your word that you'll go straight."

Bargain

"Can't do that, Governor," Cassidy answered with a grin, "I'd just have to break my word if I did. But I'll promise you this: if you let me out of here, I'll never do another job in the state of Wyoming."

Butch Cassidy was as good as his promise. Never again did he carry out a hold-up in Wyoming, even though he still used the Rocky Mountain state as his headquarters for raids and robberies throughout the rest of the far-flung western frontier.

In fact, Cassidy's favourite hide-out was the infamous Hole-In-The-Wall, a hidden valley in Wyoming's Big Horn Mountains. The Hole-In-The-Wall remained an outlaw camp for many years. Behind a great natural fortification of rocky cliffs, bands of hunted men found sanctuary from the law and created a community of desperadoes which existed on the proceeds from stolen cattle and bank hold-ups.

It was here that Butch Cassidy master-minded the activities of his outlaw gang which came to be known as the Wild Bunch.

Wild Bunch

Far and wide the Wild Bunch ranged, often in a band of as many as 100 riders. They terrorised bankers, railroad men, mining camp operators and ranchers across nearly one-third of the North American continent. With a curious blend of camaraderie and crime, Cassidy's gang carried out hold-up after hold-up with such dash and daring that the Wild Bunch became a legend in its own time.

Once in Denver, Colorado, Butch and a partner walked calmly into one of the city's largest banks and informed the president that they knew of a plot to rob his institution. "Good heavens," said the startled banker, "how did you happen to know about this plot?" "Because we planned it," replied one of the bandits and proceeded to relieve the bank of 21,000 dollars.

On another occasion, five robbers waylaid a train and demanded money from the safe. When the expressman, even with a pistol pointed at him, refused to open the strong-box, the Cassidy gang seemed perplexed. "Shall we kill him or not?" asked one gunman. "Let's vote," suggested another.

In the best democratic tradition, they voted to let the trainman go his way, bade the engineer and crew a cheery good night and rode off.

Ruthless

Although Butch Cassidy himself seemed to regard his career of crime as a sort of good-natured game, some of his henchmen were not so benevolent. There was Flat Nose George Curry, as brutal and ruthless a criminal as any in the annals of the west, and the notorious Harve Logan whose murderous temper cost the lives of dozens of frontier citizens.

During the last decade of the 19th century, the Wild Bunch alternately terrorised and delighted the inhabitants of the Rocky Mountain region. Cassidy grew into a romantic figure and his exploits were often compared with those of the legendary Robin Hood.

In point of fact, Butch Cassidy did bring a touch of genius to his nefarious trade. He may have been the first criminal in America to devise the technique known as the "protection racket".

Exorbitant

Cassidy simply offered his services for an exorbitant fee to prosperous ranchers to protect their stock against rustling. If a rancher declined the offer, his cattle would, indeed, begin to disappear, stolen, of course, by the "protector" himself.

There is no way of knowing just how many bank robberies and hold-ups Butch Cassidy master-minded during his hard-riding career. But it is certain that his ill-gotten gains could be counted in hundreds of thousands of dollars.

Time though was running out for

the western outlaw in the early 1900s. The forces of law and order began to prevail on the frontier. Perhaps Butch Cassidy was intelligent enough to recognise the trend or perhaps he simply wearied of living the life of a hunted man. At any rate, he vanished from the scene in 1902. Police officers following the trail of the notorious bandit tracked him as far as New Orleans where he was said to have boarded a steamship bound for South America.

Invasion

The next year, posses of lawmen invaded the famous Hole-In-The-Wall headquarters and either shot or arrested the remnants of Cassidy's hard-riding, fast-shooting Wild Bunch.

The conclusion of the Cassidy saga remains shrouded in mystery to this day. Some accounts say that Butch, renegade to the end, killed himself in South America, after a running battle with Bolivian police. Others hold that Cassidy returned to the scene of his crimes as an old man in 1936 searching the Wyoming mountains for a 70,000 dollar cache of gold which he had hidden many years before.

In any case, the era of the fast gun ended with the disappearance of Robert LeRoy Parker, alias Butch Cassidy, from the western frontier.

With a curious blend of camaraderie and crime, Cassidy's gang carried off hold-up after hold-up!

THE GHOSTLY GUARDIAN
part 2
CONTINUED FROM PAGE 47
ONLY TRAP, LUNGING TO THE RESCUE OF HIS YOUNG MASTER, SAVED JIM FROBISHER FROM A BARRAGE OF BLOWS!
AAARG! SHOO! GERROFF! YE PESTERIN' BRUTE!
NO, TRAP... DOWN, BOY!
GRRRRR!
RUN! GO ON! GO AND FIND FIREBRAND! FIND HIM!
FIREBRAND..?
NNNNHRRRRR!
AS THE DOG MADE OFF ALONG THE BEACH...
SO YOU'VE MADE A PAL ALREADY, EH? WELL, THIS FIREBRAND, WHOEVER HE IS, WON'T SAVE YOU, MY LAD! WE'LL BE 'EADING FOR 'OME BY THE TIME 'E GETS 'ERE!
B-BUT, HOW DID YOU FIND ME? HOW DID YOU KNOW I'D BE IN BENZANCE?
OLD ALF AIN'T SUCH A FOOL AS HE LOOKS, HEH, HEH! YOU NEVER KNEW THAT I USED TO SEARCH THAT OLD SATCHEL OF YOURS FROM TIME TO TIME, DID YER? JUST TO MAKE SURE YOU WASN'T GETTING UP TO ANYTHIN'...!
THAT'S HOW I FOUND THAT OLD PHOTOGRAPH OF MASTHEAD MANOR, WHERE YER DAD USED TO LIVE! I ALLUS THOUGHT YOU'D MAKE FOR THERE, IF EVER YOU DECIDED TO RUN AWAY..!
WELL, YOU CAN FORGET ABOUT MASTHEAD MANOR... AND YER PRECIOUS FATHER! I'VE TOLD YOU A THOUSAND TIMES, HE AIN'T NEVER COMING BACK! HE'S GONE FOR KEEPS, SEE?
NO, HE HASN'T! I..I'LL NEVER BELIEVE THAT! LET ME... GO!
JIM'S STRUGGLES WERE USELESS IN THE GRIP OF HIS POWERFUL GUARDIAN!
IF EVER I NEEDED OLD FIREBRAND, IT... IT'S RIGHT NOW! TRAP'S JUST GOT TO FIND HIM! HE'S GOT TO..!
REX CINEMA
NEWS
SPORTING CRISTAL'S
FAIR & CIRCUS FUN
DE LA TORRE IN ACTION!
AT THAT MOMENT, THE INTELLIGENT DOG WAS STILL ZIG-ZAGGING THROUGH THE STREETS OF BENZANCE ... AS IF FOLLOWING SOME INVISIBLE, GHOSTLY TRAIL!

UNTIL...
RRAAARFF!
FIREBRAND HAD BEEN OUT SEARCHING FOR JIM AND WAS NOW FEELING MISER-ABLE...
WISH THE LAD WOULD HURRY BACK! IT GETS LONELY WHEN HE'S NOT AROUND!
NEXT INSTANT...
GRRR-AUUUUF!
WAAAAAH! IT'S THAT 'ORRIBLE GREAT 'OUND-DOG!
THE STARTLED GHOST WAS INVISIBLE TO EVERYONE EXCEPT TRAP!
THE DANGED CRITTUR MUST 'AVE FOLLOWED ME GHOSTLY VIBRATIONS! YAAAH! CUT OFF, YE MANGY BRUTE! YOU COME ANYWHERE NEAR ME WOODEN LEG, AN' SO 'ELP ME I'LL...!
THEN FIREBRAND BEGAN TO REALISE THAT HIS PEG-LEG WAS NOT IN ANY DANGER!
ARF! ARF! WAAF! GRRRR!
UUHH? WH-WHAT'S THIS? FIRST, IT TURNS TAIL, THEN IT COMES BACK AGAIN! WELL, REEF ME TOPS'LS...!
THE CRAFTY CUR BE TRYIN' TO TELL ME SOMETHIN'! AND... WHERE'S JIM? BY THUNDER, THAT'S IT! THE YOUNG MASTER MUST BE IN TROUBLE!
WAAARF!
LEAD THE WAY, ME HEARTY! UP THE FROBISHERS! FIREBRAND TO THE RESCUE! WAH-HAAAR!
HECTIC MOMENTS LATER, AS THEY CAME WITHIN SIGHT OF BENZANCE RAILWAY STATION...
THERE HE IS, BY GLORY... TIED UP TO SOME HULKING GREAT LANDLUBBER! RECKON 'TIS TIME OLD FIRE-BRAND WENT A-HAUNTIN'..!
BY NOW, JIM FROBISHER HAD ALMOST GIVEN UP HOPE!
SO MUCH FOR THAT PRECIOUS FRIEND OF YOURS! HEH, HEH! WE'LL SOON BE ON THE TRAIN FOR 'OME, MY LAD! THEN YOU'RE GOING TO PAY FOR PUTTING ME TO ALL THIS TROUBLE!

THE LITTLE STATION WASN'T VERY BUSY AT THAT TIME OF THE DAY!
HOY! IS EVERYONE ASLEEP AROUND 'ERE? OPEN UP! I WANT SOME TRAIN TICKETS!
RAP!! RAP!
THE ONLY TICKET YOU'LL GET, IS TO DAVY JONES' LOCKER, YE KNOCK-KNEED SON OF A FOUR-EYED SEA-COOK!
WUUUAAAHH!
WITH A FLASH, A BOOM AND A ROAR, THE GHOSTLY SEAMAN MATERIALISED!
UNHAND THAT BOY IN THE NAME OF THE FIGHTING FROBISHERS!
S-STONE ME...!
EEEEEK!
YIPPEEEE! GOOD OLD FIREBRAND!
SO THIS IS YOUR INFERNAL FRIEND! RIGHT, MATE... YOU'VE ASKED FOR IT! NO DIRTY RAGGED OLD SEA-TRAMP IS GOING TO POKE HIS NOSE INTO MY BUSINESS!
NOT REALISING THAT FIREBRAND WAS A GHOST, ALF HUDSON LUNGED TO THE ATTACK!
THAT STUPID CUTLASS DOESN'T FRIGHTEN ME! I'LL TEACH YER TO LEAD MY WARD ASTRAY, YOU OLD HARBOUR-RAT!
H-HARBOUR-RAT? ME..?
ALF HUDSON'S FLAILING FIST MET NOTHING BUT THIN AIR!
THE CHEEKY JACKANAPES! 'TIS AN INSULT TO ME REPUTATION! A SLUR ON THE NAME OF FROBISHER!
WH-WHAT THE..?
MY GOSH! UNCLE ALFRED IS GOING STRAIGHT THROUGH FIREBRAND!
KRRR-AAAK!
HE'S DECIDED TO APPLY FOR TRAIN TICKETS ARTER ALL! GET GOING, JIM... RUN FOR IT!
AAAOWWW!
AS JIM AND TRAP DASHED OUT INTO THE STREET...
MMMPH! GET ME OUT OF HERE! HAAALP! DO SOMETHING!
RECKON 'TIS TIME I MADE MESELF SCARCE!

THAT... FIREBRAND CHARACTER MOVED FASTER THAN I EXPECTED! BUT HE WON'T DODGE ME A SECOND TIME! OUT OF MY WAY..!
AND HERE'S WHERE I GIVE YOUNG JIM A CHANCE TO FIND A HIDING-PLACE! HEH, HEH!
SCREEEEK!
PROPELLED BY FIREBRAND'S GHOSTLY ENERGY, THE LUGGAGE-TROLLEY HURTLED FORWARD!
'ERE, WHAT THE FLAMIN..? OH, N-NO!
THWUUMP!
HAPPY LANDINGS, SHIPMATE!
THWAAAANG!
WAAAAAH!
LOOK OUT! WHAT'S THAT CRAZY FOOL UP TO..?
GROOOOGH!
HEY, GET IN THE QUEUE, YOU ILL-MANNERED LOUT!
COME BACK! YOU 'AVEN'T PAID FOR THAT STEAK AND KIDNEY PIE!
THE TREACHEROUS BLIGHTER! FLUUM! SNEAKED UP BEHIND ME LIKE A PERISHIN' GHOST, HE DID! JUST WAIT 'TIL I GET ME 'ANDS ON 'IM!
HALF-DAZED, THE INFURIATED ALF DASHED FROM THE STATION, AND...
HEY! LOOK WHERE YER GOIN', YOU CLUMSY GREAT IDIOT!
CLUMMMPF!
AAAARGH!
IT'S BAD ENOUGH TRYING TO FIND SOME FUN IN THIS DUMP, WITHOUT BEING TRAMPLED ON BY IDIOTS LIKE YOU! FOR TWO PINS, I'D..!
NO... W-WAIT A MINUTE, LADS! I'LL F-FIND YOU SOMETHING TO DO!
THE ANGRY THUGS PAUSED AS HUDSON WENT ON DESPERATELY!
I WAS CHASING SOMEONE! A... A LITTLE WRETCH OF A BOY, AND AN OLD TRAMP WHO'S TRAINING HIM TO BE A THIEF! THEY'VE JUST STOLEN ME LIFE'S SAVINGS!
EH..?

I'LL BET THEY'RE MAKING FOR THEIR HIDE-OUT... AN OLD HOUSE, UP ON THE CLIFFS! YOU 'ELP ME TO CATCH 'EM, AND THERE'LL BE TEN QUID IN IT FOR YOU!
TEN QUID, EH? THAT'LL JUST ABOUT PAY FOR OUR OUTING!
LEAD THE WAY, OLD MATE..!
HUDSON AND THE TOUGHS MADE OFF... UNAWARE THAT THEIR QUARRY HAD BEEN HIDING ONLY A FEW FEET AWAY!
GOSH, THAT'S TORN IT! WHAT ARE WE GOING TO DO, FIREBRAND? WHEN THEY FIND OUT THAT WE'RE NOT AT THE MANOR, THEY'LL JUST SIT THERE AND WAIT FOR US!
AAAR!
RRAAAARF!
BUT NOT IF WE GET THERE BEFORE 'EM, SHIPMATE! COME ON! THE FROBISHERS AIN'T BEATEN YET!
BACK DOWN THROUGH THE HARBOUR AND OUT ALONG THE ROCKY BEACH HURRIED THE STRANGE TRIO!
FIREBRAND, ARE YOU SURE YOU KNOW WHAT YOU'RE DOING? WHERE ARE WE HEADING FOR?
THE MOUTH OF A CAVE, ME LITTLE MATEY! 'TIS ONLY VISIBLE WHEN THE TIDE BE OUT, AND THEN ONLY TO THEM THAT KNOWS WHERE TO LOOK!
AND SURE ENOUGH...
FEAST YER EYES ON THAT, ME HEARTY—THE BACK DOOR TO MASTHEAD MANOR!
G-GOSH!
THE CAVE-MOUTH MERGED INTO A TUNNEL, THAT WOUND UP THROUGH SOLID ROCK!
IT LOOKS LIKE AN OLD SMUGGLERS' TUNNEL... HUNDREDS OF YEARS OLD! BUT HOW DID YOU KNOW IT WAS HERE, FIREBRAND?
THERE'S, ER... N-NO TIME TO GO INTO THAT NOW, LAD! KEEP GOIN'..!
HECTIC MOMENTS LATER, AS FIREBRAND'S GHOSTLY AURA LIT UP THE DARKNESS...
A FLIGHT OF STEPS... AND A TRAPDOOR! I'LL BET IT OPENS OUT INTO THE CELLAR OF MASTHEAD MANOR!
JIM FROBISHER WAS RIGHT!
YIPPEEEE! GOOD OLD FIREBRAND!
HA-HAAAR! YOU AIN'T THE FIRST SHIP I'VE GUIDED SAFELY HOME TO PORT!

BUT I'D BETTER GET TOPSIDE! THEM LILY-LIVERED SWABS SHOULD BE TACKING OVER THE HORIZON AT ANY MOMENT...!
MOMENTS LATER, AFTER FIREBRAND HAD MATERIALISED IN THE CROW'S NEST, HIGH ABOVE THE ROOF OF MASTHEAD MANOR...
AND THERE THEY BLOW! WAH-HAAAR! SAIL RIGHT IN, YE SCURVY LANDLUBBERS! BY THE TIME I'VE FINISHED, YE'RE GOING TO WISH YE'D NEVER HEARD OF MASTHEAD MANOR!
BUT JIM FROBISHER WASN'T FEELING SO CONFIDENT!
OLD FIREBRAND MAY MANAGE TO FRIGHTEN THEM OFF, TRAP! BUT WE'VE ALSO GOT TO CONVINCE ALF HUDSON THAT I'VE LEFT BENZANCE... THAT I'M NEVER COMING BACK TO THE MANOR! OTHERWISE, WE'LL NEVER BE RID OF HIM!
COR! IT'S A... S-SPOOKY SORT OF PLACE, AIN'T IT?
YEAH! WOULDN'T SURPRISE ME IF IT.. IT WAS 'AUNTED!
RUBBISH! YOU'LL FIND NOTHING IN THERE EXCEPT MY WARD, AND THE OLD SEA-TRAMP HE'S BEFRIENDED! COME ON...!
DON'T FORGET... THERE'S TEN QUID IN IT FOR YER IF WE CATCHES 'EM! YOU THREE SEARCH THE GROUND FLOOR, WHILE I TAKE A LOOK ROUND UPSTAIRS!
OKAY, MATE..!
JIM FROBISHER WATCHED WITH BATED BREATH, AS THE THREE THUGS DREW CLOSER TO HIS HIDING-PLACE!
WE'D BETTER SEE IF ANYONE IS HIDING OUT THE BACK..!
FIREBRAND, WHERE ARE YOU? FOR PETE'S SAKE, DO SOMETHING!
AND THEN...
AH-HAAAR! GOOD EVENIN', SHIPMATES! WELCOME TO MASTHEAD MANOR!
UUHHHH? M-MY STARS..!
LET ME BE YOUR GUIDIN' 'AND, AS I TAKE YE ON A TOUR OF THIS QUAINT ESTABLISHMENT!
IT... C-CAN'T BE! I'M SEEING THINGS!
I KNEW THIS PLACE WAS 'AUNTED! LEMME OUT OF 'ERE!

BUT THERE WAS NO ESCAPE FROM THE GHOSTLY PRESENCE OF FIREBRAND FROBISHER!
BE YOU LEAVIN' SO SOON? BUT YOU AIN'T SEEN THE DUNGEONS, YET..!
WAAAAAH!
WE GOT A NICE SELECTION O' THUMB-SCREWS, AN' RACKS, AN' OTHER INTERESTIN' INSTRUMENTS O' TORTURE..!
WE'RE T-TRAPPED! THE 'EAD'S IN FRONT, AND THE 'AND'S BEHIND US!
THIS WAY! IT'S OUR ONLY CH-CHANCE..!
BUT AS THE FRIGHTENED THUGS ALMOST FELL THROUGH AN INNER DOOR...
AVAAAST THERE, YE NOISY SWABS! YE'RE KEEPIN' ME LEGS AWAKE!
OH, N-NO! NO..!
AAAAARGH! KEEP IT AWAY..! HELP!
HAH-HAAAAR!
CRAAASH!
WHIZZZZZZZ
SPLOSH!
LOOK AT 'EM, JIM, LAD! THEY WON'T STOP RUNNIN' 'TIL THEY HITS THE SEA! BOARDERS REPELLED WITHOUT LOSSES!
GOOD OLD FIREBRAND!
AND NOW FOR THAT PESKY GUARDIAN O' YOURS! WHERE IS HE?
UPSTAIRS, FIREBRAND! BUT, LISTEN..!
YOU WON'T FRIGHTEN ALF HUDSON AS EASILY AS THE OTHERS! AND WHAT'S MORE, WE'VE GOT TO CONVINCE HIM THAT HE'S JUST WASTING HIS TIME, SEARCHING FOR ME IN MASTHEAD MANOR! OTHERWISE, WE'LL NEVER BE RID OF HIM..!
MEANWHILE, UPSTAIRS...
IT'S NO USE TRYING TO HIDE FROM ME, BOY! I KNOW YOU'VE COME BACK 'ERE, TO YOUR FATHER'S OLD HOME! SHOW YERSELF, OR I'LL..!

HE AIN'T HERE! THE YOUNG SCALLYWAG HAS SUFFERED THE FATE OF ALL LANDLUBBERS WHO'VE SET FOOT IN ME STRONGHOLD!
UUHHH? WHO SAID THAT..?
BAAA-OOOOOOM!
CREAK!
RATTLE!
'TIS THE GHOSTLY GUARDIAN! AYEEEE! THE BOY HAS GONE... PERISHED, I TELL 'E! ONLY HIS... SPIRIT REMAINS, TO HAUNT MY DOMAIN!
A..S-SPIRIT? WHAT D'YER MEAN? WHERE'S THAT VOICE COMING FROM..?
AND, NEXT INSTANT...
UUUAAAAHHH! GROAN! WAIL! BEWARE THE.. GHOSTLY.. GUARDIAN..!
SO THERE YOU ARE, YOU YOUNG RIP! TRYING TO TRICK ME INTO THINKING YOU'RE A SPOOK, EH?
WELL, YOU CAN'T FOOL ME WITH ALL THAT GHOST STUFF! I'LL DEAL WITH YOU FIRST, AND THEN THAT OLD TRAMP! C'MERE..!
BUT AS ALF HUDSON MADE A GRAB FOR THE BOY...
OWWWW-OOOORRR!
S-STONE ME! WAAAW!
BEWAAARE, ALF HUDSON! SAAAVE... YOURSELF..!
HE.. HE'S WALKIN' ON AIR! FLOATIN' AROUND LIKE A PERISHIN' LEAF..!
ONLY JIM FROBISHER, AND FIREBRAND, KNEW WHAT WAS REALLY HAPPENING!
LEAVE... MASTHEAD MANOR! BEFORE THE GHOSTLY GUARDIAN GETS YOU ...TOO...'
HEH, HEH! IT'S WORKING A TREAT! THIS'LL REALLY CONVINCE THE SWAB THAT YOUNG JIM IS A GHOST!
BUT THE STUBBORN, INFURIATED ALF STILL REFUSED TO BELIEVE HIS OWN EYES!
GHOSTLY GUARDIAN, BE BLOWED! IT'S SOME KIND OF TREACHEROUS TRICK! IT'S GOT TO BE...!

GOSH, IF HUDSON GRABS ME, HE'LL KNOW I'M NOT A GHOST! OUR WHOLE PLAN WILL BE RUINED!
GAAAH! YOU MUST BE DANGLIN' ON WIRES, OR SUMMAT! BUT I'LL SOON FIND OUT, YOU CRAFTY YOUNG RIP...!
THEN...
YAAAOWWW!
WRENNHCH!
GOOD OLD TRAP! HE'S MADE HUDSON LOSE HIS BALANCE, BY TUGGING THE CARPET FROM UNDER HIM!
AS ALF HUDSON WENT FLYING INTO A PILE OF RUBBISH...
AAA-AAARGH!
HEH, HEH! THIS WAY, JIM, LAD! QUICK AS A FLASH NOW!
WH-WHAT THE-?
CLUNK!
SWIFT SECONDS LATER...
THE PERISHIN' FLOOR SEEMS TO BE MOVIN' NOW! BUT I'LL BET THAT'S JUST ANOTHER OF YER TREACHEROUS TRICKS! YOU JUST WAIT 'TIL I... UUUHHH? S-STONE ME..!
THERE WASN'T A SIGN OF JIM FROBISHER!
BUT, HE... HE WAS RIGHT 'ERE A SECOND AGO! HE... MUST 'AVE NIPPED OUT OF THE ROOM WHILE I WAS SPRAWLING IN THE CORNER! YEAH, THAT'S IT...!
BUT ALTHOUGH HUDSON DASHED INTO THE HALL, AND SEARCHED ROOM AFTER ROOM!
NOT A SIGN OF THE LITTLE BRAT! B-BUT 'OW COULD HE 'AVE MOVED SO FAST? UNLESS.. NO! I.. I WON'T BELIEVE IT! HE..HE CAN'T BE A GHOST!
THE STARTLED ALF DIDN'T KNOW IT, BUT JIM FROBISHER WAS LURKING ONLY A FEW FEET AWAY!
HE'S HIDING AROUND HERE SOMEWHERE! HE MUST BE..!
HEE, HEE! LISTEN TO HIM, FIREBRAND! IF ONLY HUDSON KNEW THAT I'D VANISHED THROUGH A SECRET TRAPDOOR!
AYE! THIS OLD PLACE BE FULL OF 'EM, SHIPMATE!
BUT THAT SWAB OUT THERE DON'T KNOW IT! AND NOW THAT WE'VE GOT HIM THINKIN' THAT YOU JUST MIGHT BE A SPIRIT, WE'LL START TO PUT THE PRESSURE ON, HA-HAAAR!
MOMENTS LATER...
BAAA-OOOOOM!
RATTLE!
CLANG!
WUUUAAAAAAH!
GROAN!
THERE'S THAT... 'ORRIBLE CRASHIN' AND S-SCREAMIN' AGAIN! WH-WHAT'S 'APPENIN'? WHO'S THERE..?
THEN...
RRRRRRG!
J-J-JIM'S DOG... FLOATING AT ME! JUST LIKE THE L-LAD WAS..!

AAAOWWW! GERROFF! K-KEEP AWAY..!
GNAAAARG! SNAP! SNARL!
TCHA! 'TIS ONLY FOR JIM'S SAKE THAT I CAN BRING MESELF TO EVEN TOUCH THE PESKY BEAST!
BUT THERE WAS NO RESPITE FOR THE NOW BADLY-SHAKEN MAN!
THE BOY'S OLD SATCHEL... B-BOBBING AROUND LIKE A FEATHER!
JIM, WHERE ARE YOU, LAD? SPEAK TO YOUR OLD UNCLE..!
BLOINNK!
HE BE IN THE LAND O' SPIRITS... A VICTIM OF THE GHOSTLY GUARDIAN! AND NOW 'TIS YOUR TURN!
RATTLE!
CHINK!
YEEEEEEK! THOSE CHAINS..!
THE CHAINS WRAPPED THEMSELVES AROUND THE SOBBING HUDSON, AS IF FILLED WITH A LIFE OF THEIR OWN!
YOU BE BEYOND ALL 'ELP NOW, MATEY! THE 'AND OF FATE DRAWS NEAR..!
IT... AIN'T 'APPENIN'! GROAN! IT CAN'T BE! HAAAAALP!
TROUBLE IS, I DON'T KNOW WHETHER TO BASH YE ON THE BONCE WITH THIS CANNON BALL...
...OR SLIT YER GIZZARD WITH ME CUTLASS..!
...OR KICK YE TO DOOM WITH ME WOODEN LEG!
OH, NO! NNNNNO..!
BWAAAAAAM!
OR ON SECOND THOUGHTS, MAYBE I'LL SPARE YER WORTHLESS HIDE... AS A WARNIN' TO ANYONE ELSE WHO MIGHT BE TEMPTED TO INVADE MY DOMAIN!
I'LL W-WARN 'EM, MISTER! SOB! I'LL DO ANYTHING! ONLY PLEASE D-DON'T HURT ME..!
BUT REMEMBER... IF YE BREATHE ONE WORD TO ANYONE ABOUT WHAT'S 'APPENED TO THE BOY, IT'S GONNA LOOK PRETTY FISHY, YOU BEIN' HIS GUARDIAN, AN' ALL! FOLKS MIGHT START THINKIN' THAT IT WAS YOU WHAT DONE AWAY WITH HIM!
I... W-WON'T SAY A WORD! GULP! I P-P-PROMISE!
A SNAP OF FIREBRAND'S FINGERS, AND...
THE CHAINS! THEY'VE...!
BLIP!
...RETURNED TO THE REALM OF GHOSTS, FROM WHENCE THEY COME! NOW GET GOIN', YE SCURVY LANDLUBBER..!